Gra:

Healthy Graze Craze Recipes to Kick start your Metabolism

Introduction / Bonus Offer

I want to thank you and congratulate you for purchasing the book, "Graze: Healthy Graze Craze Recipes to Kick start your Metabolism."

Did you know that eating small healthy meals throughout the day could actually boost your metabolism and help you lose weight while eating large meals with several hours in between could slow down your metabolism?

Having many small meals ensures you never get too hungry, which enables you to make healthier food choices, avoid overeating and stabilize your sugar levels throughout the day.

This book focuses on the amazing concept of grazing that can effectively boost your metabolism. If you are interested in learning more about grazing, then this is the right book for you. You will learn what it is, how to get started, some tasty grazing recipes you can try, a sample meal plan and so much more.

Thanks again for purchasing this book. I hope you enjoy it!

As a thank you, I'd like to offer you a **completely 100% free** workout video which can be obtained by clicking this link **here!!!** Healthy eating when combined with exercise creates the best results. I think you will really find this helpful.

Also, by Paul Dowling

Keto Diet: Cook Ketogenic Diet Recipes for Beginners

Self-Discipline: Mental Habits of Life Fulfillment and Positive Thoughts

© Copyright 2019 - All rights reserved.

This document is geared towards providing exact and reliable information in regards to the topic and issue covered. The publication is sold with the idea that the publisher is not required to render accounting, officially permitted, or otherwise, qualified services. If advice is necessary, legal or professional, a practiced individual in the profession should be ordered.

- From a Declaration of Principles which was accepted and approved equally by a Committee of the American Bar Association and a Committee of Publishers and Associations.

In no way is it legal to reproduce, duplicate, or transmit any part of this document in either electronic means or in printed format. Recording of this publication is strictly prohibited and any storage of this document is not allowed unless with written permission from the publisher. All rights reserved.

The information provided herein is stated to be truthful and consistent, in that any liability, in terms of inattention or otherwise, by any usage or abuse of any policies, processes, or directions contained within is the solitary and utter responsibility of the recipient reader. Under no circumstances will any legal responsibility or blame be held against the publisher for any reparation, damages, or monetary loss due to the information herein, either directly or indirectly.

Respective authors own all copyrights not held by the publisher.

The information herein is offered for informational purposes solely, and is universal as so. The presentation of the information is without contract or any type of guarantee assurance.

The trademarks that are used are without any consent, and the publication of the trademark is without permission or backing by the trademark owner. All trademarks and brands within this book are for clarifying purposes only and are the owned by the owners themselves, not affiliated with this document.

Table of Contents

Introduction/Bonus Offer

What Is Grazing?

Breakfast Recipes

Lunch Recipes (Meals From 12.30 Pm – 4 Pm)

Dinner Recipes (Meals Between 6.00 Pm And Your Bedtime)

Snacks and Desserts

Sample Meal Plan

   Week 1

   Week 2

   Week 3

Conclusion

What Is Grazing?

Grazing is a term used to describe the consumption of tiny, frequent meals throughout the day, usually every three to four hours. This term, however, does not refer to eating snack foods constantly, but rather, consuming your daily calories and all your necessary nutrients over five or six small meals- instead of two or three large ones.

By grazing, you are able to avoid two negative feelings, which are feeling famished or starving, and feeling stuffed or uncomfortably full.

The food can be anything you like, as long as it is healthy. After eating, you should feel satisfied and before you graze again, you want to feel, without regret. Grazers don't have to wait to be desperately hungry to eat, like typical dieters.

I know you are desperate to know how grazing meals look like, but before we plunge into the recipes, I have to mention something:

When you eat frequently, you are able to maintain your energy levels. According to research, one of the greatest benefits of eating frequently is keeping your blood sugar levels stable. The study below, for instance, shows a strong correlation between a grazing eating style with lower levels of fasting insulin, which is something that usually indicates that the body has a healthy blood sugar function and the metabolism is fine.

The blood glucose roller-coaster people usually feel when they are dieting or taking fewer meals and consuming them in huge portions can lead to weight gain, issues with blood sugar control, type 2 diabetes and insulin resistance.

In addition to helping you maintain balanced and steady energy levels, stable blood sugar will help in balancing your appetite throughout the day, thus reducing your chances of eating unhealthy foods –which are typically high in fat, sodium and sugar on impulse and in the long run, help you maintain a healthy weight.

A good case in point is a study that was published in the Journal of the Academy of Nutrition and Dietetics. The study found that participants who ate smaller meals more often ended up recording lower total calorie intake; they also had lower BMIs and as you would expect, they were more likely to choose healthy foods compared to their counterparts who consumed fewer, larger meals.

Lastly, if you have been looking for a way to be happier, this is a great opportunity for you. When you eat fewer meals, your blood sugar drops more often, and this signals your body to excrete stress hormones such as epinephrine and cortisol, which can lead to mood and sleep problems. With grazing, you never get to a point where you are extremely hungry and this ensures stable blood sugar levels and your stress hormones are under control The more these hormones are under control, the more energized and restful at night you're likely to be.

Moreover, eating often will supply your brain with a steady stream of glucose, which goes a long way in bolstering your mental sharpness, productivity and performance.

We could go on and on about the benefits of grazing but I am sure you get the idea. Grazing supports your physical and mental health, which all of us are in constant pursuit of.

Let us now look at some tasty meals that you can try out:

Breakfast Recipes

These meals are meals you can eat from 7. 00 am – 12.30 pm.

Savory Oatmeal with Cheddar

Serves 1

Ingredients

1/4 dry quick-cooking steel cut oats

Salt and pepper

1 teaspoon coconut oil, divided

1 tablespoon finely chopped onions

¾ cup water

1 tablespoon shredded white cheddar cheese

2 tablespoons diced red pepper

Directions

<u>The stove top method</u>

Bring water to a boil and then add the oatmeal. Lower the heat a bit and allow it to cook for about three minutes, until all liquid has been absorbed. Turn the heat off and add in the cheese, while stirring; season with some pepper and salt.

<u>The microwave way</u>

You can also use a microwave. Just add the oats and water to a microwave-safe bowl. Line the dish with paper towels to catch any spills. Microwave at about 8/10 power setting at intervals of one minute for three minutes in total. If you want to have a softer texture, keep microwaving at intervals of 30 seconds. Stir the oats a bit between intervals.

When the oatmeal is ready, add in the shredded cheese, pepper and a pinch of salt.

Now add 1/4 teaspoon of coconut oil to a nonstick pan and heat over medium-high heat. Add the vegetables and cook for about 2-3 minutes, until they become soft. Spoon the vegetables over the oats and enjoy.

Berry Yogurt Smoothie

Serves 2

Ingredients

1/2 cup fresh blueberries

6 ounces plain Greek yogurt

1 whole banana

1/2 cup fresh blackberries

1 cup vanilla soy milk

Directions

Add the ingredients to your blender and pulse for 30 seconds. Stir a bit and pulse for 30 more seconds. Pour the smoothie into two glasses and serve. Alternatively, you can refrigerate until you want to serve.

Avocado Toast and Egg

Serves 1

Ingredients

1 eggs (fried sunny side up)

1/4 small avocado

Sea salt and black pepper (to taste)

1 slice of multi-grain or whole grain bread (toasted)

1/2 teaspoon lime juice

Parsley (optional for topping)

Directions

Prepare your fried egg and toast to your liking. Peel the avocado and mash it. Add in salt, pepper and lime juice.

Spread the avocado on the toast evenly and then top with the fried egg. Add any desired seasonings and serve immediately.

Enjoy!

Oatmeal Power Bowl

Serves 1

Ingredients

½ banana, mashed

1/4 cup rolled oats

1/2 cup almond milk

1 heaping tablespoon chia seeds

1/8 teaspoon cinnamon

¼ cup water

1 tablespoon ground flax (optional)

Directions

Mash the banana in a medium bowl until smooth. Add the oats, chia seeds, milk, cinnamon and water and stir until well integrated. Cover and refrigerate overnight.

Add the mixture into a pot and set the heat to medium high; bring to a simmer.

Lower the heat immediately to medium low and stir often until it is heated throughout and is thick. Stir in the flax at the end.

Serve and enjoy.

Spicy Baked Eggs with Cheesy Hash

Serves 3

Ingredients

2 teaspoons of tajin seasoning

3 tablespoons of cotija cheese

1 tablespoon of sliced jalapenos, optional

3 large eggs

½ medium avocado

¼ cup of Mexican blend cheese, shredded

½ teaspoon of garlic powder

1 teaspoon of onion powder

1 teaspoon of smoked paprika

1 tablespoon of melted coconut oil

½ medium red bell pepper, diced

6 ounces of cauliflower, chopped

5 ounces of diced zucchini

Directions

Preheat the oven to about 400 degrees F then using some foil paper line a baking sheet.

Spread an even layer of cauliflower, zucchini and pepper on the baking sheet then drizzle some oil.

Season using some paprika, garlic and onion powder then stir to coat well.

Bake for around 10-15 minutes until it starts to become brown then remove the veggies from the oven and top using the Mexican shredded cheese.

Arrange sliced avocado round the roasted vegetables and crack eggs on top. Bake until the eggs are cooked for another 10 minutes then top using tajin, jalapenos and cotija cheese.

Breakfast Tacos

Serves 2

Ingredients

2 corn tortillas

2 large eggs

1/2 ripe avocado

1/4 package fully cooked mild pork sausage

1/4 cup shredded cheddar cheese

1/2 teaspoon all-purpose seasoning or salt and pepper

Salsa, Sour Cream, Lime Wedges, Fresh Cilantro for garnish

Directions

Heat your griddle to 350 degrees F. Crack the eggs and break the yolks, and season them with the all-purpose seasoning. Cook for about one minute on each side.

As the eggs cook, heat the sausage according to the package instructions.

Remove the eggs from the griddle and warm the tortillas on the griddle before it cools.

Slice the eggs into strips and layer each tortilla with some egg along with a piece of the cooked sausage, avocado and a sprinkle of cheese. Garnish with any desired ingredient and enjoy.

Smoothie Bowl

Yields 1 bowl

Ingredients

1 cup organic frozen mixed berries

2-3 tablespoons almond or coconut milk

1 small ripe banana (frozen and sliced)

To top:

1 tablespoon shredded unsweetened coconut (desiccated)

1 tablespoon hemp seeds

Directions

Add the banana and frozen berries to a blender and process on low until they become small bits. Add a little almond or coconut milk and blend on low once more, scraping down the sides as required, until the mixture attains a soft serve consistency.

Pour this into a bowl and garnish with coconut and hemp seeds; enjoy.

This smoothie is best served fresh.

Coconut Raspberry Smoothie

Serves 1

Ingredients

½ cup red raspberries

½ cup coconut cream

1/8 teaspoon coconut extract

2 teaspoons sucralose based sweetener

4 oz. silken tofu

Directions

Combine all ingredients in a blender and blend until smooth.

Pour the smoothie into a glass and garnish with cream and raspberries.

Sweet Potato Breakfast Skillet

Serves 6

Ingredients

1 red bell pepper, chopped

4 cups of diced sweet potatoes

12 ounces of bacon, cut into 1-inch pieces

1 cup of chopped onion

4 eggs

4 cups of diced zucchini

Black pepper

Additional ghee, bacon fat, coconut oil or lard

Directions

Cook the bacon pieces in a 12-inch cast iron skillet over medium low heat until crisp.

Set the bacon aside. There should be rendered bacon fat at the bottom of the skillet around 1/8 inches deep.

Preheat the oven to 400 degrees Fahrenheit then increase the heat to medium-high.

Place the diced sweet potatoes in the hot oil carefully and leave them to cook until the bottom of the cubes turn golden brown {without stirring}. Stir and cook the cubes until they just begin to soften.

Increase the heat to high then add the bell pepper, onion and zucchini to the skillet. Cook until the vegetables begin softening.

Stir in the bacon pieces then remove from the heat.

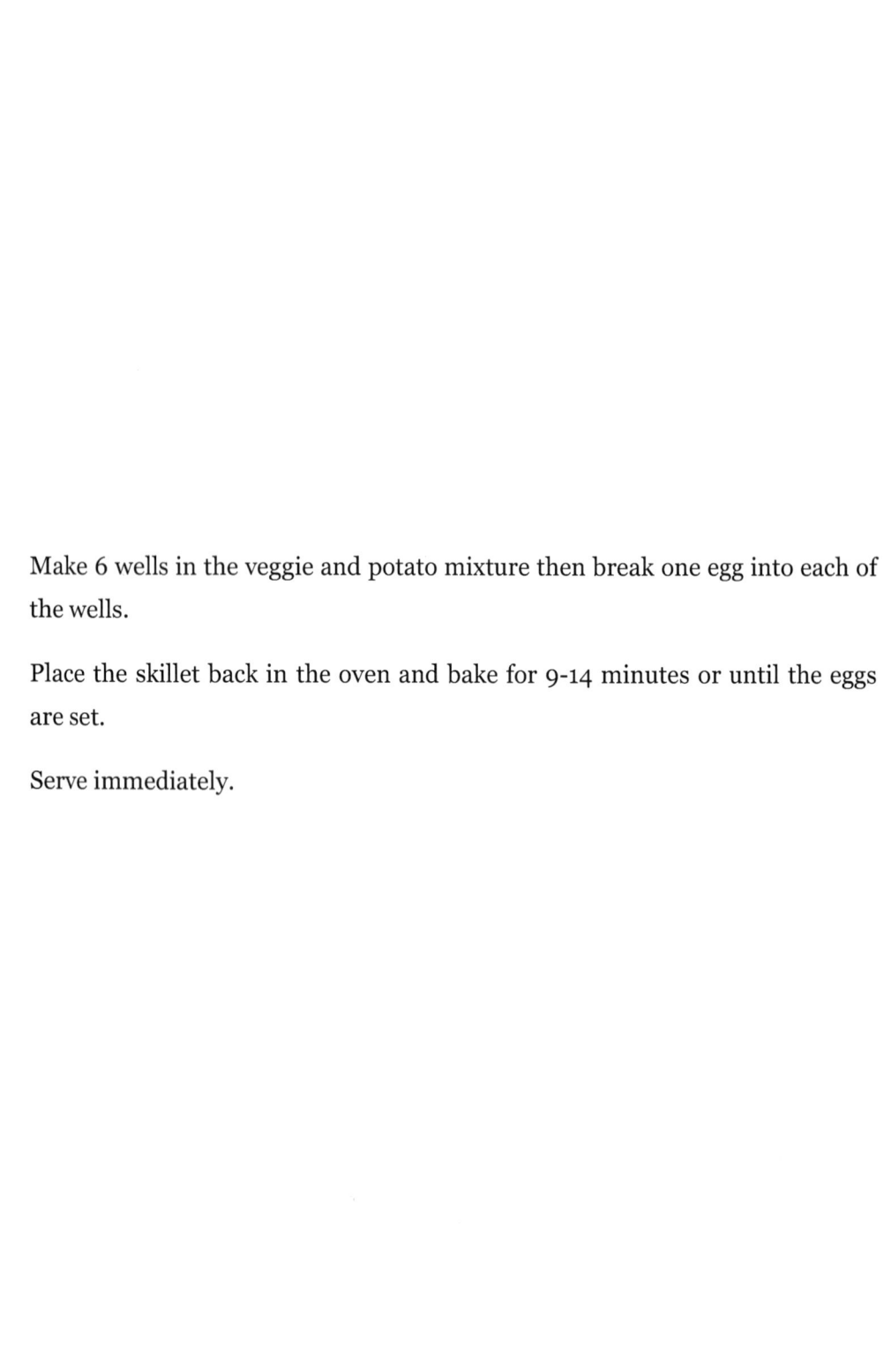

Make 6 wells in the veggie and potato mixture then break one egg into each of the wells.

Place the skillet back in the oven and bake for 9-14 minutes or until the eggs are set.

Serve immediately.

Ricotta Toast with Honey and Pistachios

Serves 1

Ingredients

Kosher salt and coarse black pepper

2 tablespoons whole milk ricotta cheese

1 slice seedy bread (or any other kind you love)

1 heaping teaspoon local honey

1 tablespoon chopped pistachios

1 tablespoon butter (optional)

Directions

Toast the bread and add ricotta cheese. Sprinkle with pistachios and drizzle with honey; finish with a pinch of pepper and salt, to taste.

Enjoy!

Quinoa Fruit Salad

Serves 6

Ingredients

1½ cup strawberries, sliced

1 mango, diced

1 cup uncooked quinoa

1 cup blueberries

1 cup blackberries

<u>Honey Lime Glaze</u>

¼ cup honey

1 tablespoon chopped fresh basil to garnish

2 tablespoons lime juice

Directions

Rinse the quinoa and prepare it according to package instructions. Allow it to set to room temperature.

Add the quinoa to a large bowl, along with the strawberries, blackberries, mango and blueberries.

For the glaze, add the lime juice and honey to a small bowl and mix. Drizzle it over the fruit salad and toss to coat.

Garnish with fresh basil.

Tutti-Frutti Muesli

Serves 2

Ingredients

½ cup nonfat or low-fat plain yogurt

¼ cup diced apple

¼ cup unsweetened muesli (see Note)

½ cup blueberries, fresh or frozen (thawed)

¼ cup diced banana

1-2 teaspoons honey or pure maple syrup

Directions

Add the apple, blueberries, yoghurt, banana, honey and muesli to a bowl and stir until well integrated.

Enjoy!

You can make this dish ahead. Just cover and refrigerate for not more than one day.

Note:

In case you've been wondering, muesli is a mixture of uncooked rolled oats seeds and nuts and fruit that's very popular in Switzerland. You can get it in the bulk section in supermarkets or with cereals.

Apple Pie Oatmeal

Serves 2

Ingredients

½ cup apples, chopped

½ tablespoon apple pie spice (see below)

1½ cups water

1 tablespoon butter

1 tablespoon brown sugar

½ cup quick oats

<u>Apple pie spice:</u>

5 tablespoons cinnamon

½ teaspoon allspice

1 teaspoon cardamom

1 ½ teaspoons nutmeg

1 teaspoon ginger

Directions

Set your pan over medium heat and add a tablespoon of butter.

As the pan heats up, chop up the apples into tiny chunks.

Put the apples in the pan and mix in with the butter. Cook for about five minutes, or until they start softening.

<u>To prepare the apple pie spice:</u>

Add the ingredients to a jar and shake thoroughly to mix. If you don't want to use apple pie spice, you can always select a simpler version, which could be simply using cinnamon.

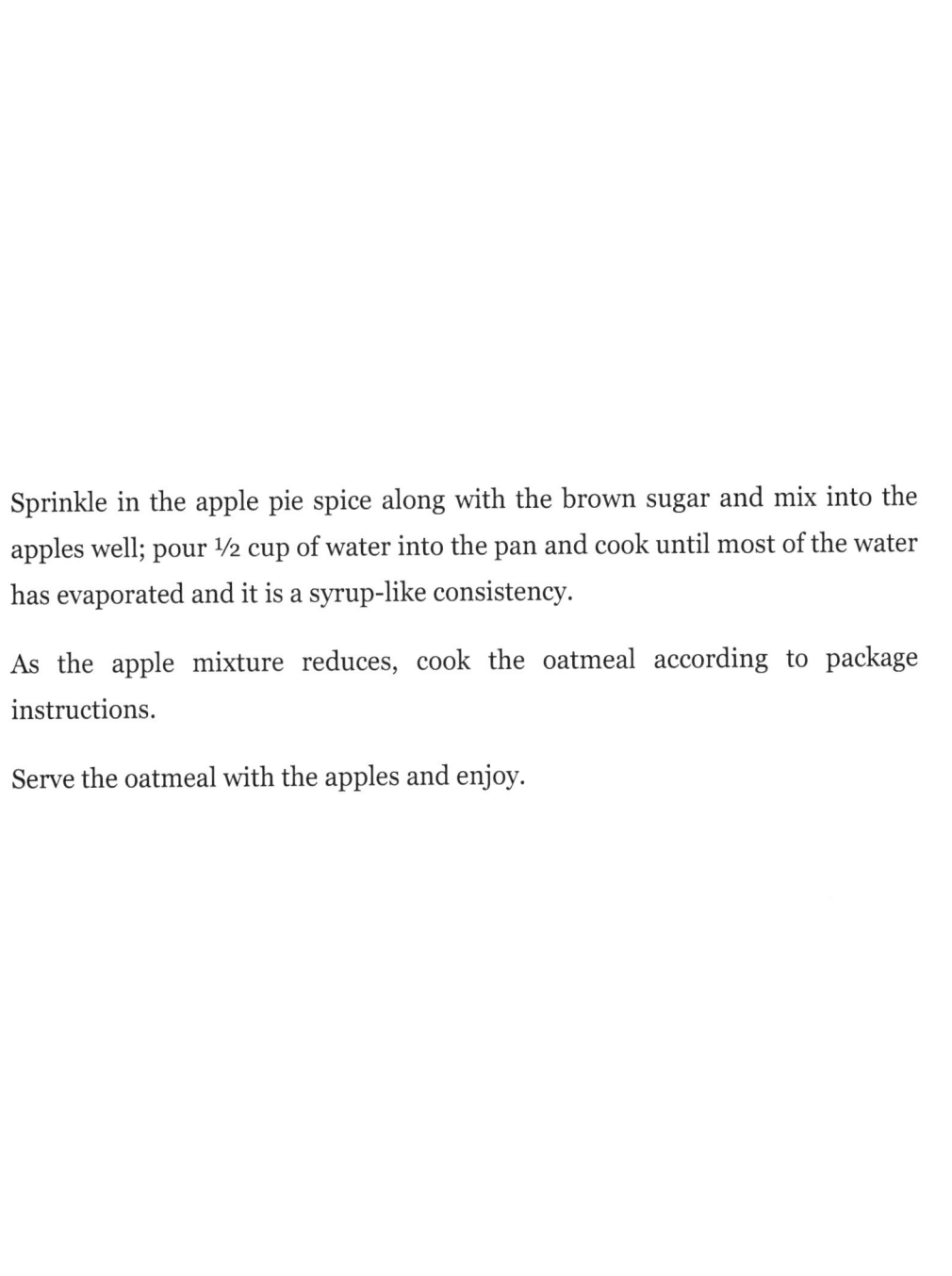

Sprinkle in the apple pie spice along with the brown sugar and mix into the apples well; pour ½ cup of water into the pan and cook until most of the water has evaporated and it is a syrup-like consistency.

As the apple mixture reduces, cook the oatmeal according to package instructions.

Serve the oatmeal with the apples and enjoy.

Maple Oatmeal with Sweet Potato

Serves 2

Ingredients

1/2 cup oatmeal old fashioned or quick

Pinch of salt

1-2 teaspoons brown sugar

Maple syrup

2/3 cup non-fat milk or low-fat if you want

1/3 cup cooked sweet potato mashed

Pumpkin pie spice

Chopped almonds

Directions

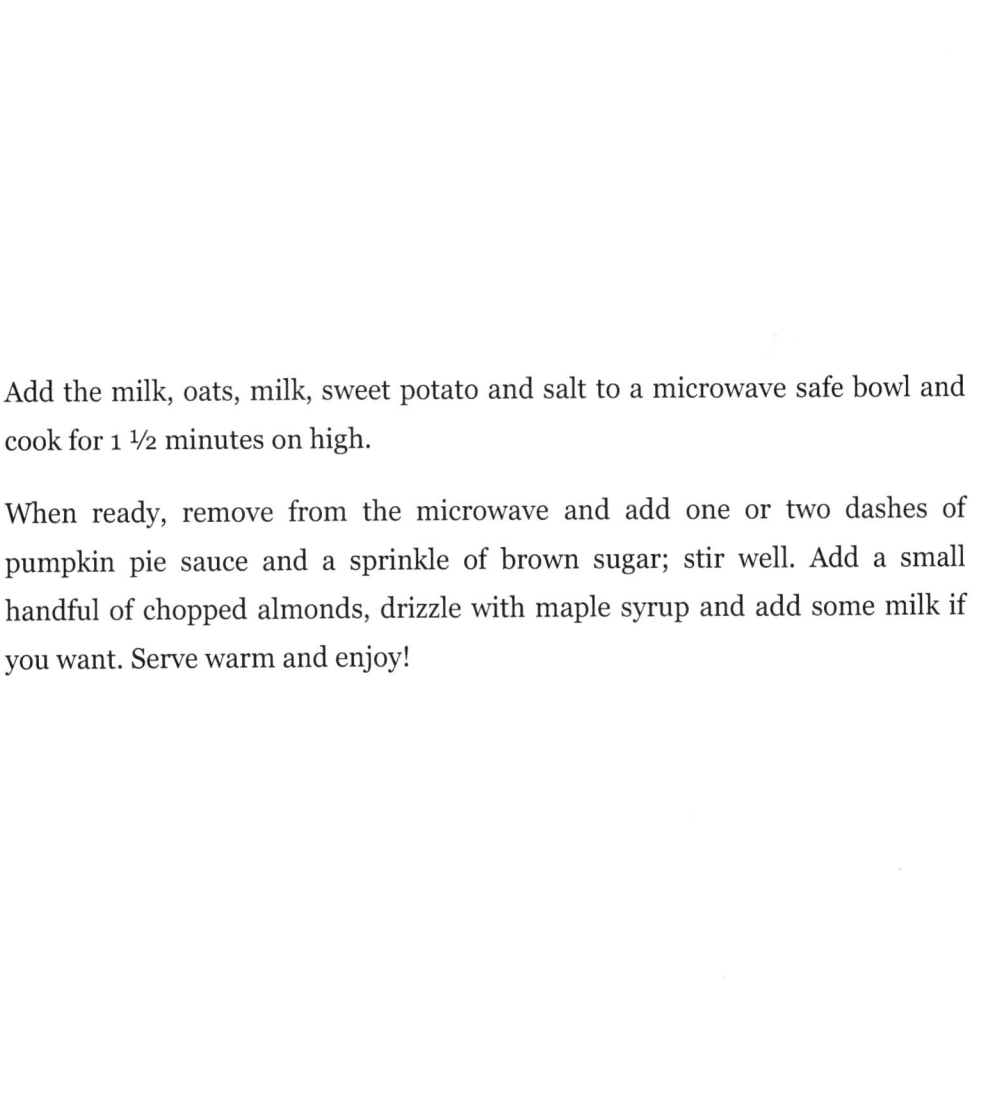

Add the milk, oats, milk, sweet potato and salt to a microwave safe bowl and cook for 1 ½ minutes on high.

When ready, remove from the microwave and add one or two dashes of pumpkin pie sauce and a sprinkle of brown sugar; stir well. Add a small handful of chopped almonds, drizzle with maple syrup and add some milk if you want. Serve warm and enjoy!

French Toast in a Mug

Serves 1

Ingredients

1 piece buttered bread

1 small egg

1 teaspoon ground cinnamon

1 tablespoon of chocolate chips

1/4 cup milk

2 tablespoons syrup

A pinch of salt

Cinnamon sugar (optional)

Powdered sugar (optional)

Directions

Get a microwavable jug and add the egg, syrup, milk, salt and cinnamon. Mix well until well integrated.

Carefully cut off the crusts of the bread and slice the bread into small, square bits.

Place the bread pieces in the mug and press them down until they become completely submerged in the liquid.

Add the chocolate to the mug and stir it a bit to have them incorporated in the mixture. If using, sprinkle the cinnamon sugar on top.

Microwave for 2 minutes, making sure to stop every 30 seconds. When ready, let it cool for 1-2 minutes.

Sprinkle the powdered sugar over it (if using), serve and enjoy.

Egg-in-a-hole

Serves 1

Ingredients

1 slice of your favorite kind of bread

Salt and freshly ground black pepper

1 tablespoon butter

1 egg

Directions

Get a glass (use the rim) or a biscuit cutter and press a hole in the middle of the slice of bread.

Set a skillet over medium-low heat and heat it to melt the butter. When it's all spread out, put the piece of bread on the butter and crack the egg into the middle of the hole.

Cook slowly until the egg sets a little on the bottom- this should take between 30 to 45 seconds. Sprinkle the egg with pepper and salt. After a while, get a spatula, flip the toast over and sprinkle the other side with pepper and salt.

Carefully transfer the entire piece of toast around the skillet, making sure it soaks up all the butter, and allow it to cook until the yolk feels soft. You want to have a nice, golden-brown toast, a white (not burned or browned) white and an unbroken yolk.

Enjoy!

Quick Bowl of Polenta

Serves 2

Ingredients

1 cup water

Pinch salt

1/4 cup coarse ground cornmeal

Milk, optional

1 teaspoon olive oil, optional

Directions

Add the cornmeal, olive oil, salt and water to a bowl and mix well. Place the bowl in the microwave, uncovered, and microwave on high for five minutes.

Remove the polenta from the microwave halfway through cooking and stir thoroughly. Add a little milk, if you want and return the bowl back into the microwave and complete the cooking time. You want it to be slightly thick.

Enjoy the dish with some more milk, along with walnuts and brown sugar. You can also top it with a poached egg.

Italian Baked Eggs

Serves 2

Ingredients

½ cup marinara sauce

1/8 cup fat free or low-fat milk

1 tablespoon freshly grated parmesan

1/8 cup basil leaves

2 large eggs

1/8 cup shredded gruyere cheese

Kosher salt and freshly ground black pepper, to taste

Directions

Preheat your oven to 425 degrees F and then apply oil to two 10-ounce ramekins or just coat them with nonstick spray.

Divide the marinara sauce among the ramekins evenly and top with the eggs, gruyere, parmesan and milk; season with pepper and salt to taste.

Put the ramekins in the oven and let the egg whites bake for about ten minutes, or until the egg whites are cooked through.

Serve immediately, and if you want, garnish with basil leaves.

Mocha Breakfast Shake

Serves 1

Ingredients

4 ounces Greek Yogurt (you can use plain or vanilla)

1 teaspoon unsweetened cocoa powder

1/3 cup milk depending on desired consistency

1 teaspoon espresso powder, instant coffee, ground coffee– anything you can grab

1 small or ½ large banana, cut into small pieces and frozen

1 scoop of protein powder (optional)

Directions

Add all the ingredients to a blender and process until smooth.

Pour into a glass, grab a nice straw and enjoy!

French Toast in a Cup

Serves 1

Ingredients

1-2 slices of bread, cubed

1 egg

Dash cinnamon

1 tablespoon butter

3 tablespoons milk

Drop of vanilla extract (optional)

Directions

Cube your bread and add your butter to a cup. Put the cup in a microwave to melt the butter and swoosh it around the cup. Add bread to the cup.

Get another cup and add vanilla, cinnamon, milk and the egg. Stir well.

Add the liquid over the bread and swoosh it a bit and let the liquid soak the bread.

Place it in the microwave and begin with one minute, and then add ten seconds in bits until it cooks to your liking- you don't want your egg runny. The total time should be about one 1 and 20 seconds. At this point, add syrup if you want and enjoy!

Breakfast Banana Splits

Serves 2

Ingredients

1 medium banana

1/2 cup vanilla yogurt

1/2 cup granola with fruit and nuts

2 maraschino cherries with stems

1/3 cup each fresh blueberries, sliced peeled kiwifruit, halved seedless grapes

Directions

Cut the banana crosswise, in a half, and then split each half lengthwise for each serving. Place on a serving dish.

Top with the rest of the ingredients and enjoy!

Honey Yogurt Quinoa Parfait

Serves 1

Ingredients

1/4 cup plain Greek yogurt

A few teaspoons honey (to taste)

1/4 cup pomegranate arils or other fruit

1/4 cup cooked quinoa

1/4 cup Cheerios

Directions

Mix the quinoa, yogurt and honey. Add ½ this mixture into a round glass and cover with ½ of the cereal and then ½ the pomegranate arils, and carefully repeat layers one more time. Serve immediately and enjoy!

Hey, can I ask a big favor are you enjoying this book? I would really appreciate it if you could leave me a review on Amazon, this way my book has more possibilities to help more people. It's simple and a link to the review can be found here. Thank you

Tasty toast

Serves 1

Ingredients

4 large blackberries, chopped

1 tablespoon unsalted peanut butter

1/2 ripe medium nectarine, diced

1 slice of bread

1 teaspoon honey (or add more to taste)

Directions

Toast the bread and spread the peanut butter on the toast evenly.

Add the blackberries and nectarines to a small bowl and spoon the fruit mixture over the toast.

Drizzle one teaspoon of honey over each slice of toast.

Easy Egg Wraps

Serves 1

Ingredients

1 egg

Optional fillings: avocado, turkey, cheese, fruit, hummus, yogurt etc

Optional seasonings: salt, paprika, pepper, basil, cayenne pepper, oregano

Directions

Set a little skillet over medium heat and grease it with oil or butter.

Crack one egg to a bowl and whisk using a fork.

Add the mixture to a hot pan and tilt the pan to spread the egg into a large circle.

Allow it to cook for a few seconds and sprinkle with seasonings if you want. Flip using a large spatula and let it cook for 30 more seconds.

Allow the egg wraps to cool a bit and top with fillings as desired. Roll and serve cold or warm.

Enjoy!

Breakfast Parfaits

Serves 1

Ingredients

1/44 cup Granola

¼ teaspoon pure maple syrup or honey for drizzling, optional

1/4 cup Seasonal fruit, such as peaches and blackberries

¼ cup whole milk yogurt

Directions

Layer the ingredients in bowls or cups and drizzle with maple syrup or honey. Enjoy!

You can also make this dish ahead and store it in your fridge. Just make sure to leave off the top layer of the granola, and then add before you serve.

Banana nut overnight oats

Serves 4

Ingredients

1/4 cup chopped walnuts, toasted

1 cup rolled oats

1 cup milk (plus some more for adding in morning)

1 large, ripe banana, mashed

2 teaspoons chia seeds

Optional: honey or maple syrup

Directions

Add the mashed banana to an airtight mason jar or container along with rolled oats, toasted walnuts and chia seeds.

Top with maple syrup, milk and a bit of added sweetener, if you're using it and stir.

Close the top and shake it properly to make sure everything mixes properly.

Put it in the fridge and let it sit for 6 hours or overnight.

In the morning, all you have to do is add some extra milk to thin out, if you want, and top with some extra chopped walnuts and sliced banana.

5-minute-Pancakes

Serves 2

Ingredients

Cinnamon or Vanilla if you like

4 tablespoons shredded oats

2 large eggs

1/2 teaspoon baking powder (optional)

1 tablespoon coconut oil (for the pan)

1 large banana

Directions

Add your oats to a blender and process them.

Mix all the ingredients together until well integrated.

Add the coconut oil to a pan. Add in the pancake dough using a spoon and cook at medium heat.

When ready, serve and enjoy!

Breakfast Burrito

Serves 1

Ingredients

Coarse kosher salt and freshly ground black pepper

1 tablespoon shredded cheddar cheese

1 egg, lightly beaten

1/8 cup baby spinach

1/2 tablespoon salsa

1 high fiber wrap or flour tortilla

Directions

Add olive oil to a small skillet or cooking spray to coat and set it over medium heat.

When the pan becomes warm, add the spinach and eggs. Cook, while stirring often until the eggs become soft and fully cooked; the spinach should be wilted as well; this should take about 2 minutes.

Remove from the heat and add salsa while stirring; season with pepper and salt.

Put the wrap in the microwave to heat for about ten seconds, until warm. Spread the cheese along the center of the tortilla evenly and add the egg mixture on top. Fold in the sides of the wrap and roll it up tightly from the bottom.

Serve immediately and enjoy!

Overnight chia oatmeal

Serves 2

Ingredients

3/4 cup unsweetened almond milk

1 tablespoon chia seeds

1/4 teaspoon vanilla

1 banana, thinly sliced

1/3 cup rolled oats

2 teaspoons honey

2 tablespoons dried cranberries, or 1 finely chopped fig

2 tablespoons toasted sliced almonds

Directions

Add the vanilla, chia seeds, oats, almond milk, honey and dried fruit to 2 mason jars and mix well.

Cover and refrigerate overnight.

In the morning, all you have to do is top with almonds and banana and enjoy.

Breakfast Sandwich

Serves 1

Ingredients

1 egg

1 slice of tomato

1 whole grain English muffin

1 slice low-fat cheese

2 leaves baby spinach

Directions

Spray a small bowl or coffee mug with oil lightly and add the egg; whisk properly and season with pepper and salt. Microwave on high, for about one minute.

Cut the muffin into two and put the tomato, cheese, spinach and egg in between and enjoy.

Savory Microwave Breakfast Mug

Serves 1

Ingredients

1/2 cup stale bread pieces

1/8 cup finely chopped vegetables

1 tablespoon butter

1 egg

1/8 cup pre-cooked chopped meat

1 tablespoon shredded cheese

1 1/2 tablespoons milk

Pinch of salt and pepper

Directions

Cut or tear the bread into pieces – each about ½ inch in size. Chop the vegetables and meat into tiny pieces and shred the cheese.

Add the butter to a large mug about 10 ounces large and microwave for 20 seconds on high, or until it melts fully. Add in the egg, milk, pepper, salt and whisk properly using a fork.

Add the cheese, vegetables and meat to the egg and milk mixture and stir properly, and then fold in the bread cubes until they are totally saturated.

Allow the mug to sit for one minute so that it absorbs the liquid fully, and then microwave on high for 90 or so seconds, or until the center is solid. Serve hot and enjoy.

Purple Smoothie

Serves 2

Ingredients

¾ cup blueberries

1/2 medium banana

2 tablespoons chopped pistachios

1 teaspoon sesame seeds

¾ cup blackberries

3 tablespoons unsweetened almond milk

1 teaspoon hemp seeds

Directions

Add the blackberries, blueberries and banana to your food processor or blender. Blend, while adding almond milk until the smoothie attains your preferred consistency. You need to note that this recipe typically makes a thick smoothie, so you may have to add a little more liquid if you want to have a thinner smoothie.

Pour the smoothie to a cup or bowl and sprinkle the hemp seeds, sesame seeds and pistachios on top and serve.

Enjoy!

Egg Muffin Sandwiches

Serves 2

Ingredients

1 English muffin, split and toasted

1 teaspoon water

Salt and pepper

1/2 teaspoon Dijon mustard

1 egg

1 tablespoon shredded cheese

1 tablespoon mayonnaise

Optional Ingredients:

Spinach

Canadian bacon

Tomato slices

Ham

Sausage

Turkey or regular bacon

Directions

Crack one egg into a microwave-safe container that is the same size as the English muffin- coffee mug would do. Add some water and beat the egg until well integrated. Add the shredded cheese over the egg mixture.

Put the container in the microwave and cook for between 35 and 40 seconds, until the liquid cooks off.

As the egg cooks, spread the Dijon mustard and the mayonnaise on all the halves of the English muffin. When the egg is finally ready, put it on top of the bread, grab the other half of the bread and top it off. You need to be careful not to take a bite too quickly as the egg will be hot.

Breakfast Mug

Serves 1

Ingredients

1 egg

Cacao or cocoa powder

1 small banana

Cacao nibs

Optional: coconut oil

Directions

Put the banana in a mug, mush it up using a fork, and crack one egg over it. Remember that the banana should be very ripe.

Add a pinch of cacao nibs, and whisk everything together using your fork. Sprinkle some cocoa or cacao powder on top.

Microwave for about 60 seconds and jiggle the mug a bit to settle. Microwave again for between 30 and 45 seconds.

Flip this onto a platter and let it cool for one second.

Enjoy!

Protein Pancake

Serves 2

Ingredients

1 medium banana

2 small eggs

1 1/2 scoops of protein powder

Directions

Add the ingredients to a bowl and whisk using a fork.

Coat your frying pan with non-stick oil and pour the batter into your pan. This batter will give you about 3 four-inch pancakes, and will be quite thin and runny, like crepes.

Flip your pancake when you notice the bubbles developing and the edges of the pancakes setting.

When both sides brown the way you want, serve on a platter and add your favorite toppings.

I topped my pancakes with strawberries, Greek yogurt, blueberries, some lemon juice and raspberries.

Enjoy!

Fluffy Waffle

Serves 4

Ingredients

1 egg

1 tablespoon sugar

1/4 teaspoon salt

¼ cup vegetable oil or melted butter

1 cup all-purpose flour

2 teaspoons baking powder

¾ cup + 2 tablespoons milk

1/2 teaspoon vanilla essence

Fresh berries, if desired

Directions

Heat the waffle iron. You may need to brush the waffle iron if it is not non-stick before you add batter for each waffle.

Add the egg to a large bowl and beat using a whisk until fluffy. Add the rest of the ingredients except the berries and beat until smooth.

Pour a little less than ¾ cup of batter onto the center of your hot waffle iron. Close the waffle iron lid and bake for five minutes or until it stops steaming. Remove the waffle carefully and repeat with the rest of the batter.

Serve and enjoy with desired toppings.

Toast with Yogurt and Smoked Salmon

Serves 2

Ingredients

2 slices country bread, toasted

4 ounces sliced smoked salmon

1 tablespoon capers

1/2 cup plain low-fat Greek yogurt

1/4 small red onion, thinly sliced

Black pepper and salt to taste

Directions

Place the toasts on a platter and divide the yoghurt evenly between them, along with the onion, salmon and capers. Finish by seasoning with pepper and enjoy!

Waffles with Nut Butter and Bananas

Serves 2

Ingredients

2 frozen whole-grain waffles

1 banana, thinly sliced

2 tablespoons almond butter or peanut butter

1 tablespoon honey

Directions

Toast your waffles according to package instructions.

Top each toast with the bananas, butter and honey and enjoy!

Banana and Almond Porridge

Serves 1

Ingredients

1/2 teaspoon chia seeds

1/4 banana, chopped

1 teaspoon almonds, sliced

1/8 cup oats

1/2 cup milk

1/2 tablespoon honey

1/2 tablespoon dates, chopped

1 teaspoon cinnamon powder

1/2 saffron thread

Directions

Soak the oats in water for a while, and then add the chia seeds to another bowl of water and let them soak for ten minutes.

Add the milk to a pan set over medium heat and let it heat up, and then add the dates, almonds, and cinnamon.

Now add the saffron thread to the milk and then add the oats after 30 seconds to cook with the milk.

When the porridge is the right consistency, and the oats are properly cooked through, which should be after one minute, remove the pan from the heat and add the porridge to a serving bowl. Add the honey to the porridge and stir through.

Garnish with chia seeds and serve.

Enjoy!

Overnight Oats

Serves 1-2

Ingredients

3/4 cup nonfat milk

1/3 cup blueberries

1/4 teaspoon finely grated lemon zest

3 drops pure almond extract

1 tablespoon toasted sliced almonds

1/2 cup old-fashioned rolled oats

1 teaspoon packed light brown sugar

1/8 teaspoon pure vanilla extract

Kosher salt

2 teaspoons honey or agave nectar

Directions

Add the oats, milk, blueberries, lemon zest, brown sugar, almond extract, vanilla and a pinch of salt to a glass pint jar or anything else you will find handy with a lid. Secure the lid and shake properly.

Store in the fridge for about 6 hours or overnight and in the morning, top with the almonds and drizzle with honey.

Tomato Avocado Melt

Serves 2

Ingredients

2 slices bread

Cayenne pepper, to taste

1/4 avocado, sliced thin

1 tablespoon mayonnaise

1/2 small tomato, sliced thin

4 slices cheese

Directions

Spread the mayonnaise on the bread thinly and then sprinkle with a pinch of pepper.

Layer the bread with the avocado and tomato slices and top them with cheese. Broil them on high for between 2 and 4 minutes, or until the bread is desirably toasted and the cheese is bubbly.

Serve and enjoy!

Lunch Recipes (Meals From 12.30 Pm – 4 Pm)

Seared Tuna Nicoise Salad

Serves 4

Ingredients

4 hard-boiled eggs, cooled and sliced

1 teaspoon of Dijon mustard

¼ red onion, sliced thinly

8 ounce tuna steak

½ cup of cherry tomatoes, halved

2 ounces of French green beans, trimmed

¼ cup of fresh basil leaves

2 mini cucumbers, thinly sliced crosswise

2 cups of petite lettuce leaves

4 radishes, thinly sliced

¼ teaspoon of kosher salt

1 tablespoon of fresh lemon juice

2 teaspoons of capers

½ garlic clove, minced

¼ teaspoon of maple syrup

1 tablespoon of extra virgin olive oil

1 tablespoon of water

Freshly cracked black pepper

Olive oil cooking spray

Directions

Bring a medium pot of water to boil then add the beans and cook until crisp-tender and bright green; for around 2 minutes. Drain then plunge the beans into ice water. Drain then set them aside.

Arrange the tomatoes, cucumbers, eggs, radishes, basil, onion, lettuce and green beans evenly in four plates.

Heat a large skillet {nonstick} over medium-high heat then coat it with cooking spray. Sprinkle the tuna with pepper and salt then place it in the pan. Cook the tuna until brown on the outside but still pink on the inside; this should take you around 2 minutes on each side. Cut thinly across the grain then arrange the tuna over the vegetables.

For the dressing, combine the lemon juice and the remaining ingredients in a small jar with a tight fitting lid. Shake well until fully combined then drizzle evenly over the salads.

Roasted Cauliflower Salad

Serves 4

Ingredients

¼ cup of fresh oregano leaves

½ cup of raisins

2 bunches of spinach

4 pork cutlets, trimmed

450 grams of cauliflower, cut into large florets

2 teaspoons of dried chili flakes

Directions

Preheat the oven to 200 degrees C

Place the cauliflower in the roasting pan and spray with olive oil. Sprinkle with some chili flakes and season. Roast for around 30 minutes or until it becomes slightly golden

Season both sides of the pork and heat the non-stick frying pan over medium heat. Spray with olive oil and cook each side of the pork for 4-5 minutes each or according to your liking. Transfer them to a plate then cover and let them rest for 5 minutes.

Place the spinach in the frying pan and cook over medium heat for a minute or until the spinach wilts; season with pepper and salt.

Combine the oregano, cauliflower and raisins in a bowl. Divide the pork and spinach among the plates then top with the cauliflower salad.

Quick & Easy Cucumber Salad

Yields about 1 cup of salad

Ingredients

1 Persian cucumber, thinly sliced

1 tablespoon white wine vinegar

1/8 teaspoon salt

1/8 cup thinly sliced red onion

½ tablespoon sugar

Directions

Peel or scrub your cucumber and slice it into thin pieces, which should be less than 1/8 inch thick.

Slice the onions thinly as well.

Put both of them in a metal or glass bowl.

Add sugar, salt and vinegar to a cup and stir thoroughly until both salt and sugar dissolve completely.

Stir the dressing into the onion-cucumber mixture and stir with a slotted spoon.

Angel Hair Casserole

Serves 2

Ingredients

1/2 teaspoon olive oil

1/2 clove garlic, minced

1/2 pound lean ground beef

3 ounces angel hair pasta

¼ cup chopped onion

1 cup sliced or diced mushrooms

12 ounce jar marinara sauce

2 ounces reduced fat cheddar cheese, shredded by hand

Directions

Preheat your oven to 375 degrees F.

Heat the oil and sauté the garlic and onions over medium-high heat for about 2 minutes. Add the mushrooms, and then cook for one minute, while stirring.

Add the beef and cook while stirring for two minutes, or until no longer pink.

Add the sauce and bring to a boil; reduce the heat and cook for five minutes, uncovered.

As the sauce simmers, cook the pasta according to the package instructions.

Spread 1/8 cup of sauce in glass measuring 1 1/8 quarts or a pyrex casserole dish.

Create two layers in the following order: drained pasta>sauce> cheese. Bake for 20 minutes, uncovered.

Caprese Fusilli

Serves 2

Ingredients

1 1/2 cups cherry tomatoes, halved

½ pound fusilli long (or spaghetti)

1 garlic cloves, minced

1/2 cup small mozzarella balls

Kosher salt and freshly ground pepper

1 1/2 tablespoons olive oil

Fresh basil, torn

Directions

Bring the water to a boil, add the pasta and cook according to packet instructions. Reserve about ¼ cup of the cooking liquid.

Heat 1 ½ tablespoons of olive oil in a medium skillet over medium heat and then add minced garlic; sauté until fragrant. This should take roughly 2 minutes.

Now add the tomato sauce to the pasta and toss to combine. Add the mozzarella, basil leaves and the pasta water you reserved in bits until the pasta is moist.

Serve and enjoy!

Quinoa Stuffed Peppers

Serves 6

Ingredients

6 medium bell peppers, tops and cores removed

3 cups cooked quinoa

1 cup good-quality salsa (I used a salsa verde with corn)

1 (12-ounce) package chipotle black bean crumbles, cooked according to box instructions

2 cups freshly shredded cheese

Optional toppings: chopped fresh cilantro, diced avocado, extra cheese

Directions

Preheat your oven to 350 degrees F. Place the peppers in a baking dish such that the cavity side faces upwards.

Add the cooked quinoa, salsa, shredded cheese and cooked black bean crumbles to a mixing bowl and stir well until well integrated. Add the mixture into the bell peppers' cavities evenly and then sprinkle the tops with the rest of the shredded cheese.

Bake, for 25-30 minutes, uncovered, or until the peppers are soft, and the cheese has melted. Top with any toppings you want and serve.

Smoked Mackerel & Leek Hash

Serves 2

Ingredients

125g potatoes, halved

1 tablespoon oil

1 large leek, thinly sliced

2 eggs

50g peppered smoked mackerel, skin removed

1 tablespoon creamed horseradish

Directions

Add a splash of water to a microwavable bowl and add the tomatoes. Cover the bowl and cook for five minutes on high. They should be tender (you can steam or simmer them).

In the meantime, add the oil to a frying pan set over medium heat and heat it; add the leeks along with a pinch of salt and cook for about ten minutes, making sure to stir often to avoid sticking, for ten minutes, until they become soft. Add in the potatoes, increase the heat and fry for a few minutes to make them slightly crispy. Flake through the mackerel.

Make two indents in the leek mixture in the pan, crack one small egg into each one and season; cover the pan and cook for around 6-8 minutes until the whites set and the yolks are runny.

Serve the horseradish as the side and enjoy!

Blackened salmon fajitas

Serves 2

Ingredients

2 salmon fillets

1/2 fajita kit

1 lime

1 tablespoon sunflower oil, or any other oil suitable for frying

1 avocado

Directions

Coat the salmon in ½ tablespoon of oil as well as the fajita spice mix. Add ½ tablespoon of oil to a frying pan and fry for 8 minutes until blackened.

Mash the avocado using a fork, season and then squeeze the juice of 1 lime. Serve the fish in big flakes with the avocado, tortillas, salsa and the remaining lime, cut into pieces.

Microwave Quiche in a Mug

Serves 1

Ingredients

1 egg

1 teaspoon melted unsalted butter

Pinch of freshly ground black pepper

1/8 cup torn pieces of fresh bread

1 teaspoon chopped fresh herbs, plus more for garnish (such as green onions, Italian parsley and chives

Pinch of salt

4 small grape tomatoes, halved

1 tablespoon grated cheese (such as cheddar cheese and mozzarella)

1 ½ tablespoons whole milk (substitutes such as half and half or heavy cream)

Directions

Add the milk, egg, melted butter, pepper, salt to a microwavable mug and whisk until the ingredients mix thoroughly, and the egg whites break up completely.

Add the bread, halved grape tomatoes, grated cheese and chopped herbs into the egg mixture, while making sure the ingredients are dispersed evenly and have not settled to the bottom of the mug.

The ingredients will remain settled within the quiche mixture properly if you avoid whisking the ingredients into the egg mixture.

Put the mug in the microwave and then cook in high for one minute, just until the egg cooks completely and the quiche is a little bit puffed.

Garnish with your favorite fresh herbs and serve.

Enjoy!

Broccoli Tots

Yields 22 tots

Ingredients

1 cup sharp cheddar cheese, shredded

1/2 cup breadcrumbs

1 bunch of broccoli, cut into equal sized florets

1/3 cup onion, finely chopped

2 eggs

Salt and pepper

Directions

Preheat the oven to 400 degrees F.

Add one inch of water to your saucepan and bring to a boil. Add the broccoli into the water, cover and lower the heat to medium. Let the broccoli cook for 5-6 minutes, or until you can easily pierce with a fork. Drain the broccoli and set aside to cool a bit.

Lay out the broccoli onto some paper towels and cover using some more paper towels. Press down on the broccoli firmly to ensure as much moisture as possible is absorbed. You can also place the broccoli at the center of a dishtowel and then wring out the water. Now chop the broccoli finely.

Add all the ingredients to a large bowl and combine them well, and then season with pepper and salt. Stir everything together until properly mixed. Fill all the muffin cups in a mini muffin tin all the way to the top, making sure to push down on the filling using your spoon, so that it is nice and compact.

Put in the preheated oven and bake for 18-20 minutes. You will see the top beginning to turn golden. To remove from the pan easily (you know, without really scratching it), run your plastic knife gently around the edges of every tot; and you will see them coming out easier.

Serve and enjoy!

Note:

If you see the tots falling apart as you take them out of the pan, you can always put them back into the oven to cook for a couple more minutes so that they become a slightly crisper or simply let them sit in the pan for a couple of minutes so that the insides become firm before you remove them from the pan.

Quinoa Fajita Burritos

Serves 2

Ingredients

1/4 cup white quinoa (uncooked)

1/2 bell pepper

3.75 ounces diced tomatoes

2 tortillas (medium to large)

1/4 onion

3.75 ounces black beans

1/4 tablespoon and 2 teaspoons taco seasoning

Vegan cheese shreds to taste

Salsa/pico de gallo

<u>Optional toppings:</u>

Avocado or guacamole, lettuce, cilantro, hot sauce, etc

Directions

Rinse and cook the quinoa according to box instructions.

As the quinoa cooks, slice the bell pepper and onion thinly. Set your skillet over medium high heat and sauté the bell pepper and onion with 2 teaspoons of taco seasoning for between 7 and 10 minutes while stirring occasionally.

When the quinoa is done, add it to a bowl. Now add the rinsed and drained black beans along with the diced tomatoes and a tablespoon of taco seasoning. Stir properly to combine.

To assemble:

Spoon the quinoa mixture, cheese and salsa, onion and pepper or any other toppings you want down the center of the tortillas. Roll them up and tuck in both sides.

Note:

If you want your tortilla or grilled burrito crispier, just toss it on a grill pan for a couple of minutes on each side before you serve.

If you want gluten-free food, you can use corn tortillas (or GF tortillas).

Lastly, if you are a lone grazer, you should freeze the burritos. Just wrap them tightly, but individually in a foil and then put them all in a sealed freezer-friendly container.

When you want to reheat them after freezing, put them in an oven preheated to 400 degrees for 25 -35 minutes, or until they are desirably heated through. If you like, finish them on the stove.

Vegetable Lo Mein

Serves 6

Ingredients

8 ounces lo mein noodles (or spaghetti, linguini, rice noodles, etc.)

1 yellow bell pepper

8 ounces mushrooms

3 garlic cloves

1 tablespoon tamari (or soy sauce)

1 small red onion

1 carrot (julienned)

5 green onions

¼ cup hoisin sauce

1 tablespoon sesame oil

Optional toppings:

Cilantro, cashews, peanuts, sesame seeds

Directions

Prepare the noodles based on the package directions and then drain; set aside. Slice the bell pepper, red onion, green onion, mushroom and then mince the garlic.

Add sesame oil to a large pan or wok set over medium-high heat.

Once the oil is hot, add the red onion, carrots, mushrooms, and bell pepper and sauté for about 4-5 minutes, or until the vegetables are crisp-tender.

Add the garlic and green onions and cook for one minute, stirring often.

Add the noodles, tamari and hoisin sauce and stir gently to combine, and then heat for 1-2 minutes.

Serve and enjoy.

Grazer's Lunch

Serves 1

Ingredients

2 tablespoons walnuts

1/4 cup raisins

1 ounce uncured deli turkey no sugar listed in ingredients

2 tablespoons cashews

3-4 dried apple rings unsweetened

1 cheese stick

1 ounce pretzels green tier

Directions

In this grazer's lunch, simply arrange all the ingredients as desired in a divided dish or several reusable containers.

Enjoy!

Hey, can I ask a big favor are you enjoying this book? I would really appreciate it if you could leave me a review on Amazon, this way my book has more possibilities to help more people. It's simple and a link to the review can be found here. Thank you

Veggie Fried Rice

Serves 3

Ingredients

1/2 block extra firm tofu, pressed and chopped into square pieces

1/2 shallot, sliced

1 stalk broccoli, chopped (or vegetable of choice)

½ cup green beans, halved (or vegetable of choice)

1/2 tablespoon rice vinegar

1 1/2 cups cooked brown rice, cold

1 tablespoon grape-seed oil (or as required)

1/2 tablespoon grated ginger

3 radishes, halved

1/8 cup soy sauce

1/2 tablespoon maple syrup

1/2 cup chopped radish greens (optional)

Optional garnish:

Chopped green onions

Cilantro

Crushed red pepper

Fresh basil

Sesame seeds

Directions

Preheat your skillet or wok on high and then spread the tofu pieces on the skillet or wok. Leave a gap of about one inch in between the pieces of tofu. You can cook in small batches if you want. Cook the tofu for three minutes, or until you notice the bottom separating from the pan easily. Flip and repeat until all sides are cooked. Now transfer the cooked tofu pieces to a wire rack or dish to cool.

Lower the heat to medium and stir in the grape-seed oil ginger, and shallot into the skillet or wok. Cook while stirring constantly for three minutes, or until the shallot becomes soft.

Stir in the broccoli, green beans and radishes and cook for five minutes, or until the vegetables are tender-crisp. Add more oil as required to avoid any sticking throughout the whole cooking process.

Whisk the maple syrup, rice vinegar and soy sauce, and pour the mixture over the vegetables. Add in the radish greens, cooked tofu and cooked brown rice as you stir and cook for five minutes, while stirring often, or until the rice is hot and begins to get crispy.

Remove from the heat and serve with sesame seeds, cilantro, basil, green onions and crushed red pepper if you want.

Note:

You can substitute between 2-3 cups of chopped seasonal veggies for the radishes, broccoli and green beans if you want.

Also, if you want a gluten-free variation, use gluten free tamari or liquid aminos in the place of soy sauce.

Vegetarian Bolognaise Hand Pies

Makes 12 hand pies (serves 6)

Ingredients

1/2 tablespoon extra-virgin olive oil

1 garlic clove, crushed

1/2 small zucchini, grated

175g roasted vegetable pasta sauce

1 small egg, lightly beaten

1/2 long red chili, seeded, finely chopped

1/2 small brown onion, finely chopped

1/2 small carrot, grated

200g lentils, drained, rinsed

2 sheets short-crust pastry, just thawed

1 x 35g sachets salsa verde

Small fresh flat-leaf parsley leaves, to garnish

Directions

Set a frying pan over medium heat and allow it to heat for a short while.

Cook the onions for five minutes, or until soft. Add the garlic and cook for 30 seconds, or until fragrant.

Next, add the lentils and zucchini and stir to combine. Add the pasta sauce and bring to a simmer. Season the dish with pepper and salt, remove from the heat and allow it to cool for 20 minutes.

Preheat your oven to 200 degrees C. Line two baking trays with baking paper.

Grab a 9 cm cutter and cut rounds from the pastry sheets. Put one teaspoon of the lentil mixture in the middle of each round and brush the edges with the egg. Fold it in half and press the edges together using a fork to seal properly. Put it in the prepared trays and brush with the egg. Bake for between 15 and 18 minutes or until golden.

Add the chili and salsa verde to a small bowl and combine well. Serve the pies with this mixture and garnish with parsley.

Enjoy!

Mini Schnitzels with Garlic Sauce

Serves 2

Ingredients

250 g skinless, boneless chicken thigh fillets

1 egg, beaten

37 g butter

100 g crème fraiche

2 tablespoons plain flour

70 g dried breadcrumbs

Mixed leaves and skinny fries (optional), to serve

2 fat garlic cloves, finely chopped

1/4 small bunch curly parsley, finely chopped

Directions

Preheat your oven to 200 degrees C. Put the chicken thigh fillets between two pieces of cling film and bash them using a rolling pin to a thickness of roughly 1 cm. Cut your chicken into bite-sized pieces and set aside.

Place the eggs, flour and breadcrumbs on three different plates. Add seasoning to the plate with the flour and toss the chicken to coat, then put into the egg and then (lastly) coat with the breadcrumbs.

Place the coated chicken on a baking sheet and cook for between 10-12 minutes.

In the meantime, melt the butter in a small pan and add the garlic. Stir while cooking for 3-4 minutes until it softens. Reduce the heat and add in the crème fraiche while whisking and then the parsley and seasoning to taste.

Serve the sauce in a little pot (that is easy to dip into) on the side, and then sprinkle the rest of the parsley over the sauce. Serve with salad and enjoy.

Avocado, Mango, and Toasted Seed Salad

Serves 2

Ingredients

1 cup torn romaine

1 cup torn baby kale

<u>Toppings</u>

1/2 cup edamame

1/2 cup sugar snap peas, sliced

1/2 cup chopped mango

1/2 avocado coated in mixed toasted seeds (pumpkin, sesame, hemp, sunflower)

<u>Soy Vinaigrette</u>

1 tablespoon rice-wine vinegar

1/2 teaspoon soy sauce

Kosher salt and freshly ground pepper, to taste

1/2 teaspoon brown sugar

2 tablespoons extra-virgin olive oil

Directions

Top the greens with mango, edamame, seed-crusted avocado and sugar snap peas so that you leave some extra space in the container to make it easy to mix.

Keep the ingredients for the vinaigrette in a small jar and shake well to mix. Add dressing to the container to avoid the wilted greens right before you eat, and then cover and shake.

Enjoy!

Rainbow Trout and Basil in Parchment

Serves 4

Ingredients

4 fillets rainbow trout

2 small tomatoes, sliced

Extra-virgin olive oil, for drizzling

Kosher salt and freshly ground pepper

1 cup fresh basil leaves, torn if large

Directions

Preheat your oven to 400 degrees F. Arrange the fillets in the middle of parchment rectangles and season with pepper and salt, before topping with tomatoes. Drizzle some oil over them, fold the parchment and place on a rimmed baking sheet.

Bake until the fish cooks through, which should take between 12 and 14 minutes.

To serve, top with basil and enjoy!

Note:

If you want some foolproof folding, try arranging the fillet in the middle of a parchment rectangle. Link the long sides up and make a couple ¼-inch folds to seal. Now fold the ends, as though you are wrapping a gift and tuck beneath.

Faux Pork Cutlet Rice Bowls

Serves 2

Ingredients

300 grams cooked rice

12 imitation katsu snacks

1 ounce mentsuyu (Japanese noodle soup base)

2 ounces water

Mitsuba

Pickled ginger

Sesame oil

1/4 onion

1 teaspoon cane sugar

2 eggs, whisked

Nori strips

Directions

Grease your muffin pan with some sesame oil and fill it with the cooked rice. Press it down using a spoon to create a pocket in the middle. Bake in the oven at 200 degrees Celsius for 15 to 20 minutes.

Set your frying pan over medium heat and combine the sliced onions, katsu snack pieces, mentsuyu, cane sugar and water. Cook until the onions are soft, and pour the eggs over it and cook for 1-2 more minutes.

Pour the cooked mixture into the rice cups and garnish with pickled ginger, mitsuba and nori.

Mini Satay Chicken Skewers

Serves 5

Ingredients

1/4 cup satay sauce

1/2 tablespoon kecap manis

1/8 cup coconut milk

5 chicken tenderloins, halved lengthways

1-2 sliced green spring onions

20 x 16 cm bamboo skewers, soaked

Directions

Add the kecap manis, milk and sauce to a large bowl and mix well. Transfer about ¼ cup to a heatproof jug and set aside.

Add the chicken to the rest of the sauce mixture in the bowl, toss to coat and thread onto the skewers.

Oil a large grill plate and set it over medium heat. Put the skewers onto the grill plate in two batches and cook for 5 minutes (or until everything is cooked through), while turning often. Remove.

Just before you serve, microwave the reserved sauce on high- that's 100% power- for roughly 40 seconds, or until hot.

Put the skewers on a serving plate and spoon over the hot sauce. Garnish with the onions

Egg Fried Rice in a Mug

Serves 2

Ingredients

1 cup jasmine rice, cooked

2 tablespoons chopped red pepper

A little bit of mung bean sprouts

1 large egg

1/2 teaspoon sesame oil

1/4 teaspoon five-spice powder

2 tablespoons frozen peas

1/2 stalk of green onion, sliced

A little bit of shredded purple cabbage

1 tablespoon soy sauce, low-sodium

1/2 teaspoon onion powder

Directions

Put the rice into two mugs and then add in the green onion, peas, mung bean sprouts, red pepper and cabbage on top. Cover the mug using cling film and then puncture two tiny holes through the film using a knife. Microwave for one minute and 15 seconds on high.

Meanwhile, beat the egg and add in the seasonings (five spice powder, onion powder, sesame oil and soy sauce) while mixing. Add the egg mixture into the mug and stir with the rice and vegetables.

Again, cover the mug using the cling film and microwave for 1 minute to 1 minute 30 seconds. Get the mug out of the microwave and stir. Allow the fried rice to stand for one minute to complete cooking. Fluff up the rice using a fork and serve.

Enjoy!

Egg and Potato Salad Pita

Serves 2

Ingredients

1 cup potatoes, peeled and diced

¼ cup green peas

2 tablespoons dill pickles, diced

2 leaves Boston lettuce

1 egg, in shell, at room temperature

2 tablespoons mayonnaise

2 pita

Salt and pepper

Directions

Add water to a saucepan and bring to a boil. Add the potatoes and cook for five minutes. Reduce the heat, add the egg and let it simmer for 10 minutes. Towards the end of the cooking, add the peas for one minute, drain and allow to cool.

Peel the egg and put it in a bowl. Now add the peas and potatoes. Crush the mixture using a potato masher, with half of the mayonnaise. Add the pickles and mix properly; season with pepper and salt.

Get a clean work surface and cut the pita in half to have two discs. Spread some mayonnaise in each pita and serve with the lettuce and egg salad.

Potato Soup in a Mug

Serves 2

Ingredients

1 cup sodium reduced chicken broth

1/4 tsp garlic powder

Salt & pepper to taste

Sour cream

Chopped green onions

2/3 cup instant potato flakes

1 cup milk

Shredded cheese

Ready-to-eat real bacon bits

Directions

Add the chicken broth to a microwave and microwave it for two minutes on high, or until it boils. Grab a fork and whisk in the garlic powder, potato flakes and milk until smooth; season with pepper and salt to taste.

Microwave on high for about 45 seconds, or until hot -but don't let it bubble. Top with cheese, green onions, bacon and sour cream.

Enjoy!

Veggie "Sushi" Rolls

Serves 1-2

Ingredients

2 organic raw sushi nori sheets

¼ organic red bell pepper, cut into thin strips

1/4 organic zucchini, cut into thin strips

1 avocado, mashed

1/4 large organic carrot, cut into thin strips

1/2 cup alfalfa sprouts

Sauce

2-4 tablespoons of nutritional yeast (depending on your taste preference)

1 tablespoon of finely chopped cilantro

1 tablespoon freshly squeezed lemon or lime juice

1-2 teaspoons of gluten free, low-sodium tamari sauce

1 tablespoons of Dijon mustard

Salt and pepper to taste

Directions

Add all the ingredients for the sauce in a small bowl and mix until they form a creamy paste. If you find the texture too thick, you can add more lime or lemon juice or water; if too thin, you can add more nutritional yeast.

To assemble:

Place the nori sheets on a flat area, a countertop or cutting board and dice, cut and mash the avocado in another bowl and set aside.

Now pour and spread half of the sauce on the closest end of the nori sheets to you. Spread half of the avocado where you spread the sauce- at the closest end of the nori sheets.

Lay the thinly sliced carrots, bell peppers and zucchini on top of the avocado, horizontally or parallel to the edge of the nori sheet. Top with alfalfa sprouts.

Take the edge with the entire filling and flip/roll over (with a steady, quick hand) until you are unable to see the "filling". Keep "rolling" until you get to the other end.

Wet your index finger with some water on the far end until the sheet is damp- this makes a "glue" of some sort to hold it together.

Complete the rolling and press the wet edge onto the remaining roll to finish.

Dampen your hand lightly with water and run alongside the entire roll to let the whole nori roll dampen a bit- this makes it easier to cut.

Repeat the steps above for another nori sheet.

Note:

You have the option of slicing these rolls into tiny bite-size pieces using a sharp knife or simply eating as two long rolls (which are preferable, particularly for a quicker meal). You can also top with sesame seeds if you want and use the remaining sauce to dip. If you want, you can also serve this with a little salad or fermented vegetables.

You are free to experiment with adding in your own ingredients. For instance, you can try quinoa, brown rice or even protein like fish or chicken.

Lemon Rosemary Salmon

Serves 2

Ingredients

1 tablespoon olive oil, or as needed

2 salmon fillets, bones and skin removed

1 lemon, thinly sliced

4 sprigs fresh rosemary

Coarse salt to taste

Directions

Preheat your oven to 200 degrees C. In the meantime, arrange half of the slices of lemon on a baking sheet in one layer. Layer with two sprigs of rosemary, and top with the fish fillets.

Sprinkle the fish with salt and add a layer of the remaining rosemary sprigs, and put the rest of the lemon slices on top. Drizzle with olive oil and bake for 20 minutes in the oven. The fish should be easily flaked with a fork.

Serve and enjoy!

Oven Baked Swai

Serves 1

Ingredients

1/2 clove garlic, minced

1-1/2 teaspoons olive oil, or as needed

1 (4 ounce) fillet swai fish

Salt and ground black pepper to taste

1/2 onion, chopped

1/2 (14.5 ounce) can petite diced tomatoes

Directions

Preheat your oven to 200 degrees C and put the fish in a casserole dish. Season it with black pepper and salt.

Place a skillet over medium heat and heat the olive oil. Add the onion and cook it while stirring until it softens, for about 10 minutes. Now add the garlic and cook for one minute, until fragrant. Pour the tomatoes over the onion mixture and cook while stirring until heated through. That should take about 5 minutes. Add the tomato mixture over the fish.

Put the fish in your preheated oven and bake it until it flakes easily using a fork; this should take about 20 minutes.

When ready, serve and enjoy!

Ratatouille

Serves 1

Ingredients

1 tablespoon olive oil

1 small zucchini, quartered lengthwise, cut into thin slices

1/8 teaspoon kosher salt

1 clove garlic, minced

1/8 teaspoon dried oregano

1/8 teaspoon freshly ground black pepper

1/2 small onion, thinly sliced

1 small red bell pepper, chopped

1 Roma tomato, coarsely chopped

1/4 teaspoon dried basil

1/8 teaspoon dried thyme

1 tablespoon grated Parmesan cheese

Directions

Set a 10-inch skillet over medium high heat and add the oil. Add the onions, zucchini, salt and red peppers. Cook for about 8 minutes, until the vegetables become a bit tender.

Add the garlic, tomatoes and spices and cook for five minutes, while stirring occasionally.

Transfer the dish to a plate and add parmesan cheese on top.

Garnish and serve. Enjoy!

Macaroni and Cheese

Serves 1-2

Ingredients

2 ounces elbow macaroni

1 tablespoon all-purpose flour

1/2 cup sharp cheddar cheese, shredded

1/8 teaspoon kosher salt

1 tablespoon butter

1/2 cup milk

1/8 teaspoon dry mustard

Directions

Prepare the pasta according to the box instructions, drain and set aside. Melt the butter in a small saucepan set over medium-high heat.

Add the flour and cook for one minute, while stirring often.

Add in the milk while whisking slowly but constantly, and cook for 4-5 minutes until the mixture becomes thick and there are no visible lumps.

Add in the cheese while stirring, along with the dry mustard and salt, and keep on stirring until the cheese melts completely.

Remove from the heat and add in the pasta while stirring,

Serve immediately and enjoy!

If you want, you can also wait for it to cool but remember the macaroni and cheese thickens as it cools.

Quick Ramen Bowl

Serves 2

Ingredients

1 package ramen noodles

3 medium button mushrooms

1 large egg, optional

1 cup fresh spinach

2 whole green onions

1 teaspoon chili garlic paste

Directions

Add two cups of water to a small pot and bring to a boil. As you wait for the water to boil, prepare the vegetables by washing and slicing them.

When the water starts boiling, put in the noodles and prepare them according to the box instructions (you should ideally boil them for five minutes). Now add the seasoning or if you prefer to consume less sodium, use half a packet; stir until completely dissolved.

Reduce the heat to medium and add in your desired fresh vegetables while stirring. Let them sit in the hot broth for between 1 and 2 minutes, or until they become slightly soft.

Create a well in the middle of the pot and add the egg into it. Let the egg poach in the broth until the whites are clearly solid- the yolk should still be runny.

If you want, you can break the yolk and stir the pot a bit to have egg ribbons, as is the case in egg drop soup. At this point, water should not be boiling, otherwise the egg will dissolve into tiny pieces which will generally make the broth cloudy.

Add the soup to a bowl and enjoy with a splotch of chili garlic paste.

Cacio e Pepe

Serves 1

Ingredients

3 ounces pasta of choice, spaghetti or bucatini

4 tablespoons unsalted butter

1/4 cup reserved pasta water

12-14 black peppercorns

1 tablespoon extra-virgin olive oil

1/4 cup finely grated Pecorino, plus more for garnish

Directions

Add water to a medium pot, add the salt and bring to a boil. Add in the pasta and cook slightly, just before al dente. The pasta will cook later for 1-2 minutes. Drain the pasta in a colander and reserve ¼ cup of the pasta water and set the two aside.

Toast the peppercorns in a medium skillet until fragrant, for 2-3 minutes. Transfer them to a mortar and pestle and crush them until coarse.

If you want, you can also transfer the peppercorns to a pepper grinder or just wrap them in a plastic wrap and crush them thoroughly with the back of the skillet (one that is not hot).

Melt the butter in the same skillet set over medium heat and add the olive oil. Add a couple pinches of pepper, two tablespoons of pasta water and cheese and stir constantly until the cheese melts and the sauce begins coming together; takes about 2 minutes. Reduce the heat to medium low, add the pasta to the skillet and toss a bit in the sauce until it's coated evenly. The cheese will be clumpy a bit. Stir the pasta vigorously with a fork for one minute or so, until no longer clumpy. If the pasta is a bit dry, add one or two teaspoons of pasta water until you get a desirable consistency.

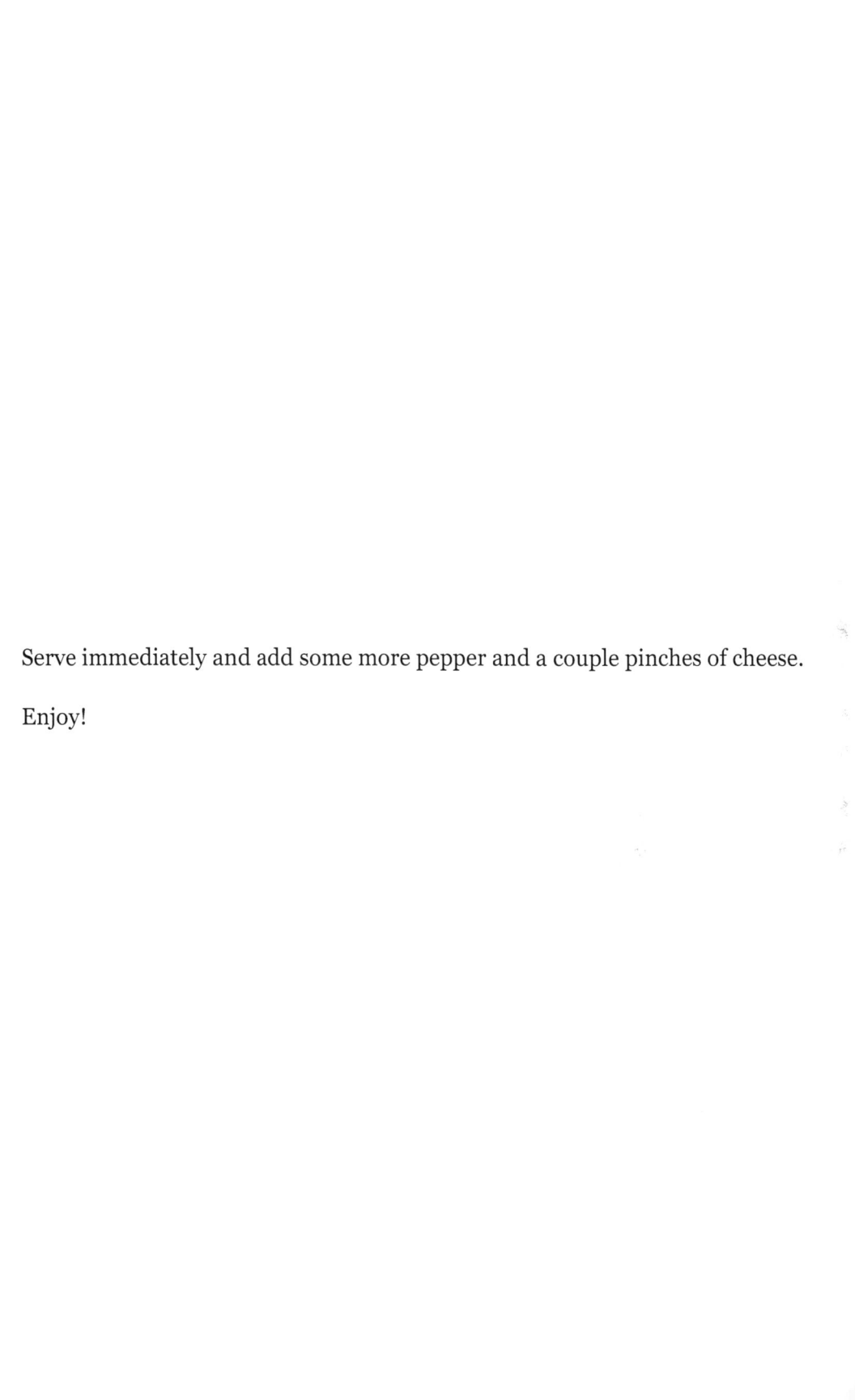

Serve immediately and add some more pepper and a couple pinches of cheese.

Enjoy!

Tasty Cauliflower

Serves 1-2

Ingredients

1 whole cauliflower

The marinade:

75g fresh ginger, peeled

1 teaspoon chili flakes

15g parsley

180ml olive oil

2 heaped tablespoons suya spice (see below)

2 cloves garlic

1 teaspoon salt

15g fresh oregano (leaves stripped from one big stalk)

200g white onion (half a large onion), quartered or roughly chopped

Spice Blend:

½ teaspoon ground cloves

½ teaspoon ground cinnamon

1 tablespoon smoked paprika

½ teaspoon ground nutmeg

1 tablespoon ground ginger

½ teaspoon salt

Directions

Mix all the ingredients for the spices and store any leftovers in an airtight container.

Preheat your oven to 180 degrees C. Meanwhile, blend the marinade ingredients together until smooth.

Prepare the cauliflower by removing the outer leaves and set aside. To obtain an extra side, wash the leaves, remove the woody ends and blanch them in boiling water for up to two minutes. Drain and sauté with one tablespoon of olive oil and another of butter, a good punch of suya spice and salt and one clove of garlic.

Separate the cauliflower into florets, and cover them with the marinade, making sure to get it into as many crevices as possible. Put it in a casserole dish or a lined baking tray, cover, and refrigerate as you wait for the oven to heat. Remove from the fridge about five minutes before you roast the florets and bake for about 35 minutes.

You can add some extra veggies such as parsnips, turnip tops and carrots if you double the marinade, to have a nice roast vegetable medley.

Serve and enjoy!

Chicken Bruschetta Pasta Salad

Serves 1

Ingredients

1/2 cup boiled pasta, drained (about 60g dry weight)

1 tomato, finely chopped

1 small chicken breast, pre-grilled and seasoned with Seasoning (or any garlic powder or seasoning of choice)

Drizzle of balsamic glaze

1/2 red onion, finely chopped

Fresh basil leaves, finely chopped

1 teaspoon garlic olive oil

Directions

Add the tomatoes, onion and pasta to a bowl and mix well, add the oil and combine, and then season with a bit of salt, to your taste.

Now top with chicken and a drizzle of balsamic glaze.

Serve and enjoy!

Note:

At this point, you can also sprinkle some parmesan cheese on top.

Fresh Mozzarella and Basil Sandwiches

Serves 2

Ingredients

2 slices toasted whole wheat bread

3 thick slices fresh mozzarella

5-6 fresh basil leaves sliced

Salt and pepper to taste

2 teaspoons balsamic glaze

1/2 tomato sliced

1 tablespoon olive oil

Directions

Drizzle half of the balsamic glaze on a slice of bread. Add the tomatoes, mozzarella and basil.

Drizzle olive oil on top and the remaining glaze, and season with pepper and salt. Add another slice of bread and cut it in half.

Enjoy!

Minestrone Soup

Serves 2

Ingredients

2 strips bacon

1 clove garlic, minced

1/2 cup canned red beans, rinsed and drained

3/4 cup frozen mixed vegetables

1/2 teaspoon kosher salt

1/2 cup small pasta

1/2 cup chopped onion

1/2 teaspoon Worcestershire Sauce

1/2 cup canned diced tomatoes

2 cups chicken broth

1/4 teaspoon black pepper

Directions

Slice the bacon into pieces each ¼ inches thick and cook them in a pot set over medium heat; stir occasionally until crispy. Remove the bacon from the pot and put it on a plate lined with paper towel.

Add the chopped onions to the pot and cook them for 2-3 minutes until they become translucent. Add the minced garlic and cook for one more minute.

Add in the Worcestershire sauce, the diced tomatoes, red beans and the mixed vegetables, stir for one minute.

Add the chicken broth and add the cooked bacon while stirring.

Season with some pepper and salt and let it boil gently.

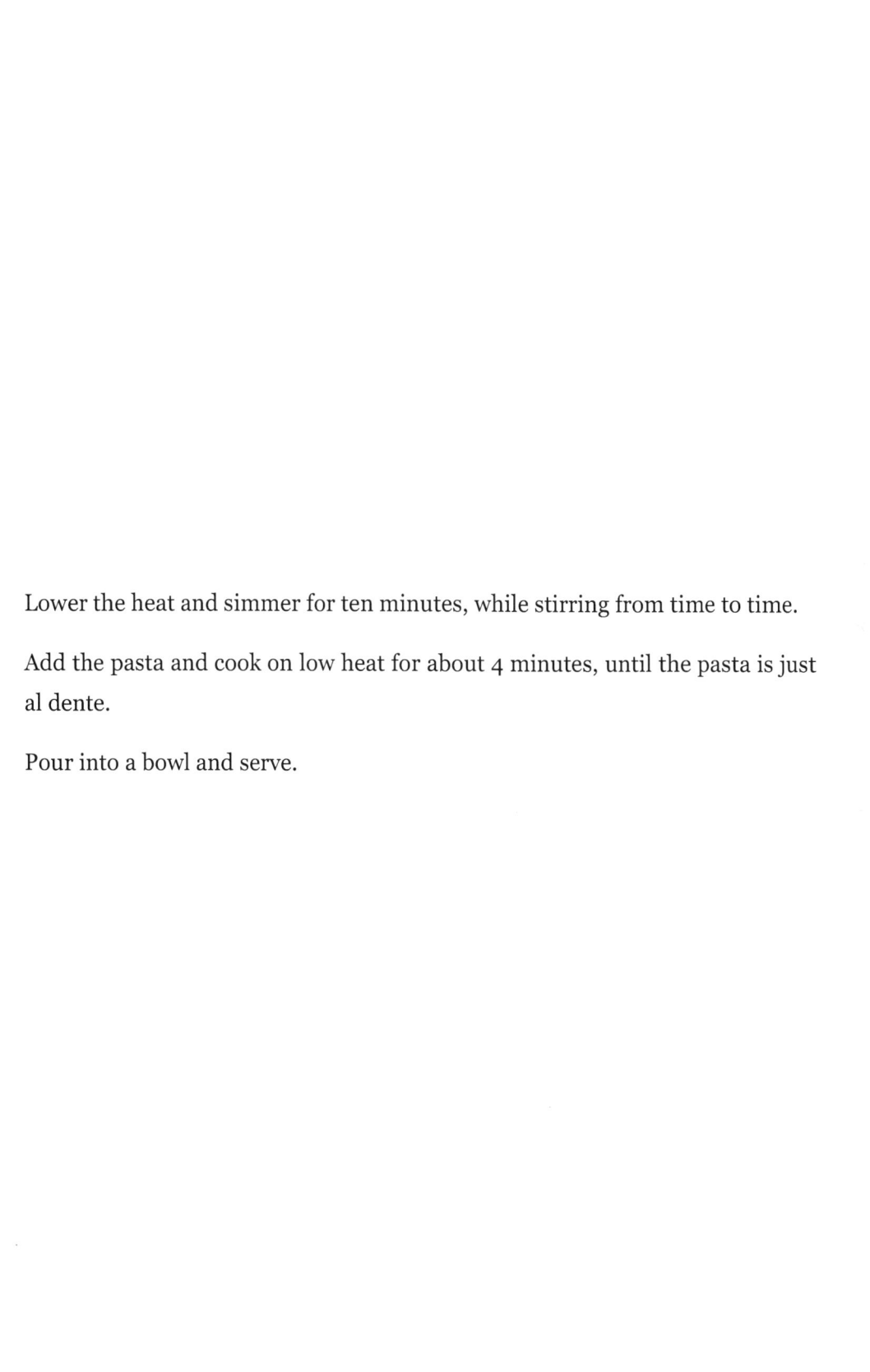

Lower the heat and simmer for ten minutes, while stirring from time to time.

Add the pasta and cook on low heat for about 4 minutes, until the pasta is just al dente.

Pour into a bowl and serve.

Dinner Recipes (Meals Between 6.00 Pm And Your Bedtime)

Miso Udon Soup

Serves 1-2

Ingredients

100g dry noodles

1 instant miso soup sachet

1 teaspoon soy sauce

2 spring onions (scallions)

1 egg

250ml water

4-5 chestnut mushrooms

Sesame seeds to serve

Directions

Prepare the noodles according to the package directions. When they are just about to get ready (about three minutes before) immerse the egg into the boiling pot.

As the egg and noodles cook, put the mushrooms on the cutting board, quarter them and then chop the onions.

Add 250ml of boiling water to your serving bowl along with the miso soup sachet, and then add the soy sauce. Stir until it completely dilutes.

Add in the mushrooms (to the broth) and set the onions aside.

When ready, drain the noodles and egg, adding the noodles to the soup before you remove the shell from the soft-boiled egg carefully. You can run it for a couple of seconds under cold water if you find it too hot to handle.

Nest the egg with the noodles and sprinkle with the sesame seeds and spring onions. Dig in and enjoy.

Note:

You may find it hard to remove the shell of a soft-boiled egg. Make sure you use a spoon to scoop it out if you are struggling to do it.

Smoky Artichoke-Sardine Salad

Serves 2

Ingredients

½ cup extra-virgin olive oil

1 large shallot, minced

¾ teaspoon smoked paprika (see Note)

¼ teaspoon freshly ground pepper

½ cup canned artichoke hearts, rinsed

¼ cup sliced red onion

3 tablespoons sherry vinegar

1 teaspoon Dijon mustard

¼ teaspoon salt

3 cups mixed greens

2 ounces canned sardines

Directions

Add the shallot, paprika, vinegar, oil, mustard, pepper and salt to a blender and process until smooth.

Put the greens in an individual salad bowl and toss with two tablespoons of the dressing. Put the rest of the dressing in your refrigerator. Add artichoke hearts, onion and sardines on top of the greens.

Tip: You can make this dish ahead by covering and refrigerating the leftover dressing for 5 days or less.

Note:

We used smoked paprika because it is made from smoke-dried red peppers and adds an earthy, smoky flavor. You can use it in different types of dishes.

Pork Chop with Pineapple Salsa

Serves 2

Ingredients

1 cup pineapple chunks

1/2 jalapeño chili

1/4 cup fresh cilantro

Ground pepper

1 bone-in pork loin chop

1/2 small red onion

1 tablespoon honey

Coarse salt

1 tablespoon vegetable oil

1 teaspoon all-purpose flour

Directions

Add the onion, pineapple, cilantro, jalapeno and honey to a medium bowl and combine; season with pepper and salt and set the salsa aside.

Add oil to a skillet set over medium heat and heat it. Meanwhile, season the pork with pepper and salt and dust with the flour. Place it on the skillet and cook until it browns on both sides, and is opaque throughout; this should take around 3-4 minutes on each side. To serve, top the pork with pineapple salsa and enjoy!

Poke Avocado Bowl

Serves 2

Ingredients

1/2 cup brown rice

3 tablespoons low-sodium soy sauce

1 tablespoon sesame oil

1 green onion, sliced

1/2 avocado, cubed

Splash of rice wine vinegar, optional

3 tablespoons ponzu sauce

1 teaspoon black sesame seeds or toasted sesame seeds, or a combination, plus more for garnish

1/2 round ahi tuna

1/2 serrano pepper, sliced thinly

Directions

Prepare the rice according to the packet directions. You can add a splash of rice wine vinegar and a pinch of salt to the rice.

Whisk together the sesame oil, soy sauce, sesame seeds, green onions and ponzu sauce.

Dice up the tuna into tiny pieces and throw them into the medium bowl with the sauce. Toss properly until coated thoroughly. Let it marinate for five minutes.

Add the cubed avocado to the tuna and toss lightly. Next, add the rice to a bowl and add the marinated tuna and avocado mixture on top. Garnish with the habanero slivers and a couple pinches of sesame seeds. Serve immediately and enjoy!

Creamy Pork Chop

Serves 1

Ingredients

1 apple

1 Pork chop

1 tablespoon Dijon mustard

A handful green beans

1 tablespoon olive oil

3 tablespoons double cream

1/4 teaspoon thyme

Directions

Set a pan and pot of water over high heat. As the pan heats up, slice and core the apple into about eight wedges, and leave the skin on. When the pan warms up, pour the olive oil and fry the pork chop for two minutes on each side, season with cracked pepper and coarse salt.

Reduce the heat and add the apple. Cook for about five minutes, while turning the fruits and chop half-way through.

Meanwhile, add the mustard, thyme and cream to a small bowl and combine. Pour the cream over the pan and toss delicately; simmer over low heat for five more minutes so that the sauce reduces, thickens and darkens.

In the meantime, prepare the green beans: season the boiling water with salt and cook the green beans.

When both are ready, serve and enjoy!

Chicken with Olives and Peppers

Serves 1

Ingredients

Olive oil

2 vine tomatoes

1/2 red pepper

1/4 teaspoon thyme, dry

6-8 olives

1 skinless chicken leg

1/2 red onion

1 garlic clove

1/2 teaspoon paprika

50ml water

Directions

Add some oil to your frying pan and heat. Season the chicken with pepper and salt, and then brown in the oil for 2-3 minutes per side.

In the meantime, chop your tomatoes and slice the pepper and onion. Add them to the pan, along with the squashed garlic clove as soon as the chicken has color on both sides, and rest the leg over the vegetables.

Reduce the heat to medium, cover with a lid and cook for ten minutes. When done, remove the lid, add the olives, spices and water. Season it with pepper and salt, stir and scrape the bottom of the pan using a wooden spoon.

Cover and cook for 5-10 more minutes, until the chicken cooks through, and the sauce thickens.

Check and adjust the seasoning and serve with a bit of fluffy rice.

Serve and enjoy!

Cod with Cauliflower Couscous

Serves 2

Ingredients

2 tablespoons water

Juice from 1/2 lemon

Olive oil

3 ounce cod filet, cleaned and pat dried

5 olives

1/2 pound head of cauliflower, cut into florets

Salt

2 carrots, sliced in half, lengthwise

Small handful of Italian parsley, minced

Directions

Preheat your oven to 400 degrees F.

Add the cauliflower florets to a food processor and process until you have crumbles.

Set a pan over low heat and add some water. Add the cauliflower into the pan and cover. Let it steam for five or so minutes, or until the cauliflower couscous soften. Add the lemon juice as you stir. Add a couple pinches of salt and mix. Taste and adjust the lemon juice and salt according to your liking, turn off the heat and cover until you're all set to serve.

Line your baking sheet with parchment paper. Lay the olives, carrots and cod filet on the baking sheet (there is no use of a cutting board here) and drizzle a teaspoon or so of olive oil over them; rub them thoroughly. Sprinkle the cod and carrots with a couple liberal pinches of salt. Put the olives and cod on a paper towel and transfer the baking sheet containing the carrots to the oven.

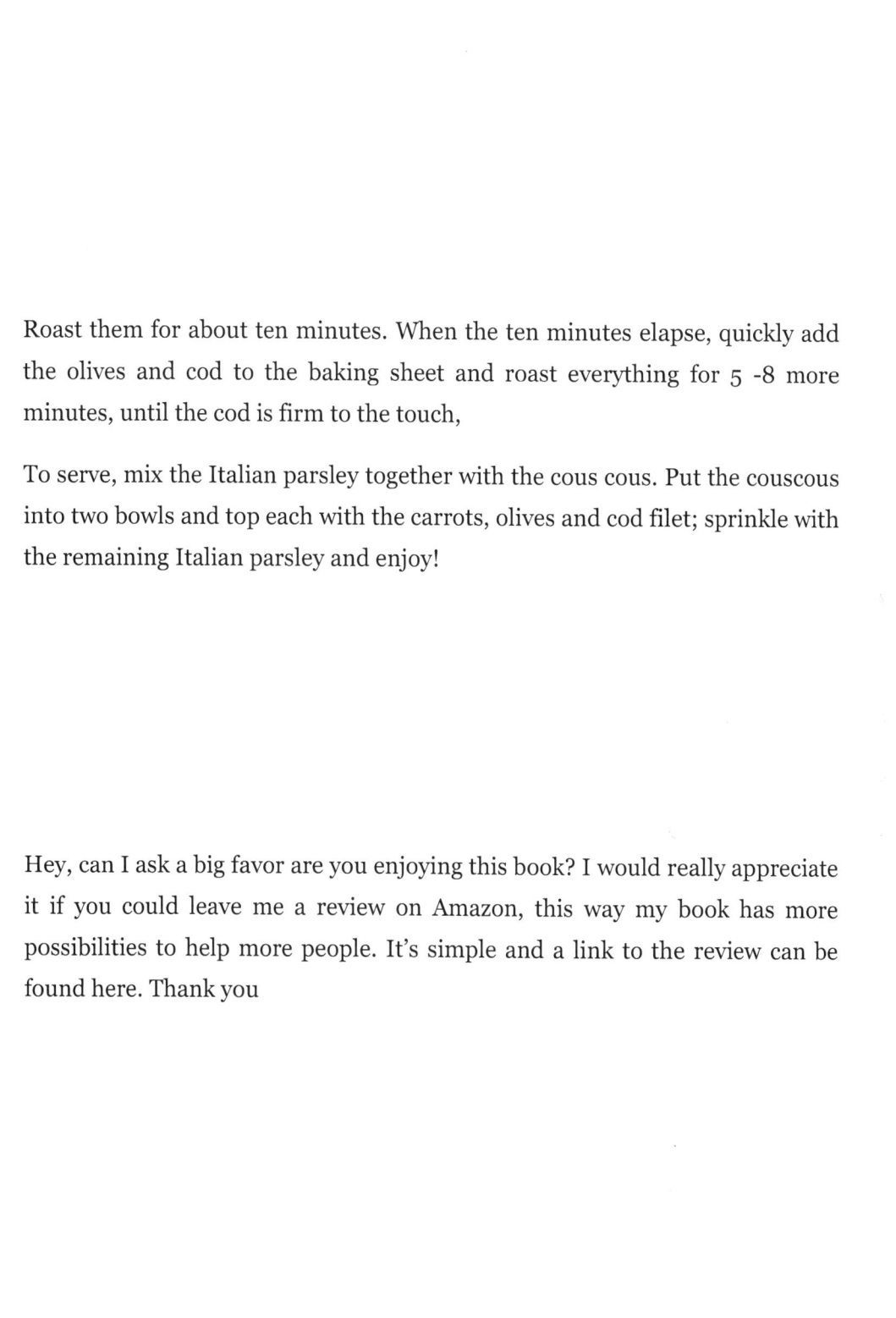

Roast them for about ten minutes. When the ten minutes elapse, quickly add the olives and cod to the baking sheet and roast everything for 5 -8 more minutes, until the cod is firm to the touch,

To serve, mix the Italian parsley together with the cous cous. Put the couscous into two bowls and top each with the carrots, olives and cod filet; sprinkle with the remaining Italian parsley and enjoy!

Hey, can I ask a big favor are you enjoying this book? I would really appreciate it if you could leave me a review on Amazon, this way my book has more possibilities to help more people. It's simple and a link to the review can be found here. Thank you

Beet Salad on a Stick

Serves 2

Ingredients

2 beets

1 log of goat cheese

2 cups arugula

½ cup California Walnuts

Honey balsamic vinaigrette:

⅓ Cup olive oil

2 tablespoons Dijon mustard

1 tablespoon honey

3 tablespoons balsamic vinegar

Salt and pepper to taste

Directions

First, roast your beets. Preheat your oven to 400 F. Slice the beets' tops (close to the root) off and scrub them nicely. Wrap the beets loosely in a foil and roast them for 50- 60 minutes.

Allow the beets to cool and rub the peel off using a paper towel.

Slice the beets into rounds, and then quarter slice them. Now put your ingredients on the skewer. Begin with two quarters of beet, followed by a bunch of arugula and finally a slice of cheese. Add the chopped California walnuts on top of the salad sticks and drizzle with honey balsamic vinaigrette.

Enjoy!

Grilled Garlic Shrimp Skewers

Serves 5

Ingredients

1 pound, 16-20 large prawns, peeled and deveined

Salt

3 tablespoons butter

3 cloves garlic, minced

1 teaspoon minced chives for garnish

Extra virgin olive oil

1/4 teaspoon kosher salt

Directions

Set up the grill and prepare it for direct high heat; one side of the grill should be the cool side without flame or coals.

Now thread the shrimp on skewers. As the grill heats up, thread the skewers through the shrimp starting at the tail and pushing the skewers through the middle and end of the shrimp. Brush the shrimps with olive oil and sprinkle with salt.

Next, melt the butter with garlic by placing the two ingredients in a microwave-safe bowl and heating them in a microwave until the butter fully melts and is hot. You can also simply melt the butter with the garlic in a little saucepan on the stovetop.

Arrange the skewers on the grill such that the shrimp are over the flame or coals and the exposed ends of the bamboo skewer are exposed and are over the cool section of the grill. Grill for approximately two minutes per side.

When ready, serve basted with garlic butter: remove from the grill and put them on a serving dish or platter. Baste them generously with molten garlic butter, and sprinkle with chives.

Enjoy!

Sweet and Spicy Tuna Salad

Serves 1-2

Ingredients

3/4 teaspoon apple cider vinegar

1/4 teaspoon garlic powder

1/4 teaspoon smoked paprika

1/2 carrot

1 (5 ounce) can tuna

1 green onion

1 teaspoon brown sugar

1 teaspoon olive oil

Pinch cayenne pepper

Pinch salt

Freshly cracked pepper

Directions

Drain the tuna properly and put it in a bowl. Grab a cheese grater and shred the carrot. Now slice the green onion as well.

Add the green onion, olive oil, carrot, apple cider vinegar, brown sugar, garlic powder, cayenne, smoked paprika some freshly cracked pepper and salt to the bowl with the tuna and stir everything until well integrated. Allow the mixture to settle for five or so minutes so that the flavors blend.

When ready, serve immediately, or refrigerate until you are all set to dig in.

Serve and enjoy!

Charred Corn and Zucchini Salad

Serves 1

Ingredients

1 ear fresh sweet corn

1/2 zucchini

1/2 ounce feta

½ tablespoon oil

1/4 red onion

Pinch of salt and pepper

1 tablespoon cilantro, chopped

Directions

Cut off the silk and husks from the corncobs; cut the stem off as well. Brush the corn's surface with some oil.

Set a grill pan or cast iron skillet over medium heat for about five minutes.

Once it's hot, add in the corn cobs and let the corn cook, and turn it frequently, until the kernels become brightly colored and develop deep char marks. This should take about 15 minutes.

As the corn cooks, slice the zucchini in half lengthwise and the red onion into thick rings. Brush all the sides of the onion and zucchini with oil.

When the corn cooks fully, place it on a chopping board to cool a bit, and then add the zucchini in its place. For about ten minutes, cook the zucchini well on each side until it is well charred, and then transfer it to the chopping board. Cook the onion as well until charred on each side- for 3-5 minutes.

Chop or slice your zucchini into quarter rounds or half rounds and then chop the onion into tiny pieces. Chop the cilantro as well and place all three ingredients in a large bowl.

Grab a sharp knife, let the cob stand and slice it down on each side carefully and remove the kernels. Add the kernels into the bowl with the onion, cilantro and zucchini.

Season the vegetables with a few generous pinches of pepper and salt, and then toss to combine. Lastly, crumble the feta on top and toss everything once more to have everything well combined. Now serve immediately, or refrigerate if you want to eat later

You can serve this salad cold or warm.

Note:

You need to use high heat oil such as safflower oil, peanut oil, avocado oil or light olive oil- which is not extra virgin.

Secondly, if you are not a fan of cilantro, you can use sliced green onion in its place here.

Lemony Artichoke and Quinoa Salad

Serves 2

Ingredients

Freshly cracked pepper

1/4 teaspoon salt

1/4 red bell pepper

1/4 fresh lemon

1/4 cup quinoa

1/4 cup chopped fresh parsley

1/4 15-ounce can chickpeas

1/4 13-ounce can quartered artichoke hearts

1/2 clove garlic, minced

1 tablespoon olive oil

Directions

Rinse the quinoa properly in a fine wire mesh sieve and add the clean quinoa into a pot with one (cup or less) of water. Cover the pot and lower the heat, and let the water come to a boil. When it reaches a full boil, reduce the heat to low and allow it to simmer for 15 minutes- with the lid on.

As the quinoa cooks, prepare the lemon-garlic dressing. Zest the lemon and squeeze the juice out. Now add the lemon juice and ¼ - ½ teaspoon of the zest to a jar or bowl along with the minced garlic, olive oil some freshly cracked pepper and salt and whisk the ingredients thoroughly until well integrated. If you are using a jar, close it and shake it well until everything combines. Set this dressing aside.

Once the quinoa cooks, spread it out on a shallow, but wide dish- a casserole dish would do perfectly here. Put it in the fridge and leave it there, uncovered for about 15 minutes to cool down.

As the quinoa cools, prepare the remaining salad ingredients. Drain the artichoke hearts and chop them roughly into tiny pieces. Next, dice the red bell pepper into fine pieces before chopping the parsley as well, roughly. Rinse and drain the chickpeas well and put them in a large bowl along with the bell pepper, artichoke hearts and parsley.

When the quinoa cools down almost completely, add it to the bowl with the other salad ingredients. Toss everything gently to combine, and then drizzle the lemon garlic dressing nicely over the top. Toss everything again gently until everything is well coated in dressing.

Serve immediately or refrigerate for up to 4 to 5 days.

Note:

You have the option of using the artichoke hearts in oil or water, with herbs or without.

Grilled Zucchini Hummus Wrap

Serves 2

Ingredients

1 cup kale, tough stems removed

1 tablespoon olive oil

1/8 cup sliced red onion

2 slices white cheddar

4 tablespoons hummus

Salt and pepper

1 tomato, sliced

2 gluten free tortillas

1 zucchini, ends removed and sliced

Directions

Heat your grill or skillet to medium heat. Remove the ends from the zucchini and slice it lengthwise into strips. Toss the sliced zucchini in olive oil and sprinkle with pepper and salt.

Add the sliced zucchini on the grill directly and allow it to cook for three minutes, making sure to turn and cook for two more minutes.

Set the zucchini aside.

Now put the tortillas on the grill for about one minute, or until you can see some grill marks and the tortillas are pliable.

Remove the tortillas and assemble wraps, a slice of cheese, zucchini slices, ½ cup of kale, onion, tomato slices and 2 teaspoons of hummus.

Wrap it properly and enjoy your wrap.

Quinoa Brown Rice Bowl

Serves 2

Ingredients

1/4 cup cooked white quinoa

1/3 cup black beans with caramelized onion

1/2 plum tomato, seeds removed and diced

1 tablespoon taco sauce

1 chopped green onion

Salt and pepper to taste

1/4 cup cooked brown rice

1/2 ripe avocado sliced lengthwise

2 soft boiled eggs

2 tablespoons salsa

1 tablespoon freshly chopped cilantro

Directions

Prepare the rice and quinoa based on the box directions. You can use ½ cup of each and a bit over one cup leftover after two servings. Dice a medium-large onion and put it in a skillet containing one tablespoon of vegetable oil; cook it on medium-low heat as you stir occasionally- this will caramelize the onion, and is meant to take between 10 and 15 minutes.

Open a 14- ounce can of black beans and place it in a strainer; rinse it. Now add the beans to the skillet with the caramelized onion, and cook for three or four minute until warmed. Slice the tomato lengthwise into quarters and remove the seeds using your thumb and dice it.

Slice ½ of your ripe avocado.

Add 4-5 cups of water to a sauce pan; add eggs using a slotted spoon or a little kitchen spider, and boil them for 5 minutes so that you have a runny yolk.

Using the slotted spoon, remove the eggs and add into ice cold water for about 30 seconds to cool them slightly; peel.

Assemble the grain bowl as you want, and drizzle with taco sauce and a pinch of pepper and salt.

Add cilantro and green onion to garnish.

Note:

For this recipe, we used regular brown rice, which takes between 40 and 45 minutes to cook. You should use a microwavable package of rice if you want to save time.

Spaghetti Pea Carbonara

Serves 4

Ingredients

4 ounces uncooked thin spaghetti

2 slices turkey bacon

1 garlic cloves minced

1 egg

1/2 tablespoon lemon juice

1/8 teaspoon dried oregano

Pinch salt and pepper

1/4 tablespoon olive oil

¼ cup onion

1/4 cup frozen peas thawed

1/8 cup milk

1/8 cup Parmesan cheese grated

1/8 teaspoon red pepper flakes

Directions

Prepare the pasta until al-dente. This should take roughly 6 minutes.

In the meantime, add the turkey bacon to a large saucepan and cook for 3 or so minutes on each side until it is well cooked through and crispy. Remove from a pan and onto paper towels. Avoid draining the grease from the pan.

Add the onion and oil to the pan you used to cook the bacon and cook over medium heat for about 2-3 minutes or until it just becomes tender.

Add the garlic and cook for some more time, turn off the heat when ready, add in the peas and stir. Chop up the turkey bacon and put it back to the pan with the onion. When the pasta cooks, add it to the pan with the onion and bacon mixture. Add in the lemon juice and milk, stir, and then the oregano, cheese, pepper, red pepper flakes and salt.

Serve immediately and enjoy!

Salmon & Couscous

Serves 1- 2

Ingredients

75 g couscous

1 handful of asparagus

2 ripe tomatoes

1 x 120 g salmon fillet, with skin on, scaled, pin-boned

½ lemon

1 small courgette

1 fresh red chili

A few sprigs of fresh coriander

Extra virgin olive oil

1 tablespoon fat-free natural yoghurt

Directions

Add the couscous to a bowl, cover it slightly with boiling water and cover it with a plate for ten minutes.

Slice the courgette nicely into batons, cut the woody ends off the asparagus; deseed the chili and chop it finely.

Chop the tomatoes roughly, and then chop the coriander leaves roughly, and discard the stalks.

Slice the salmon into small strips. Drizzle it with olive oil and season the strips with a pinch of salt and pepper.

Set non-stick frying pan over medium heat; add in the salmon and then the chili and courgette. Cook for two minutes ensuring that you turn the salmon halfway.

Add the lemon juice, tomatoes, one tablespoon of oil and the coriander to the couscous, and add black pepper and salt according to your taste.

Remove the salmon strips from the heat and onto a plate carefully, and then add the couscous to the vegetables left in the pan. Toss well to combine and then put the salmon strips over the couscous. Put a lid or tin foil on top and put it back on high heat for one last minute, or until the fish is cooked.

Serve and spoon over the yoghurt; enjoy!

Corn Soup

Serves 2

Ingredients

2 ears of corn, shucked

2 cups potatoes

Kosher salt and freshly ground black pepper

3 tablespoons unsalted butter, divided

¼ teaspoon cayenne pepper

2 tablespoons sesame seeds

Directions

Remove the kernels off the cobs and cut the cobs into two.

Add 2 tablespoons of butter to a medium saucepan set over medium heat and heat it. Next, add the corn kernels and fry for 2 or so minutes.

Add 2 ½ cups of water, the potatoes and let it boil over medium heat. Put a lid over the saucepan and let it simmer until the potatoes are tender, for between 12 and 15 minutes.

Remove the cobs and discard them, and pour ¾ of the soup from the pot into the food processor, blender or bowl. Process until smooth and then return it back to the pot with the rest of the soup. Season it with pepper and salt, and finish with the cayenne.

Now add in the rest of the butter in a small skillet set over medium heat and let it melt. When the butter starts turning golden and starts to smell nutty (takes around 6 – 7 minutes), add the sesame seeds and cook them until they turn golden brown- this should take roughly one minute.

Drizzle the soup with the sesame seed butter and enjoy!

Caramelized Onions on the Grill

Serves 1

Ingredients

2 tablespoons softened butter

Garlic salt and pepper to taste (optional)

1 large sweet onion, peeled and cut into wedges

1 teaspoon beef bouillon granules

Add all ingredients to list

Directions

Preheat your outdoor grill for medium heat. Put the onion wedges on a heavy-duty aluminum foil. Dot it with butter, and then a sprinkle of bouillon, pepper, garlic salt and pepper. Fold the foil into a packet, but leave a tiny hole at the top so that the steam escapes easily.

Put the packet on the grill and cook until the onions soften, and cooked to a deep brown; this should take between 45 minutes and 1 hour depending on the grill's temperature. After 30 minutes, stir the onions to keep them from burning.

Sheet-Pan Chicken Fajitas

Serves 1

Ingredients

100g boneless, skinless chicken breast, cut in thin strips,

2 bell peppers, sliced thinly

1/4 tablespoon fajita seasoning

1 whole-wheat tortilla

1/4 large onion, cut in thin strips

¼ tablespoon olive oil

Directions

Preheat your oven to 400 degrees F.

Toss the chicken, onion and peppers with the olive oil and fajita seasoning.

Spread it on a sheet pan in a single layer and bake for about 15 minutes; the chicken should be cooked through and the vegetables tender. Serve with tortillas and enjoy!

Kale, Quinoa, Avocado & Roast Chicken Salad

Serves 3

Ingredients

1/2 cup uncooked quinoa

2 cloves of garlic, finely chopped

A bunch of kale, washed and finely sliced

1/2 store-bought roast chicken, shredded

Salt to taste

1 cup hot water (to cook the quinoa)

1 tiny handful of flat leaf parsley, finely chopped

Olive oil (to sauté the kale and to make the dressing)

1 avocado, halved, pitted & peeled

Freshly grind black pepper

Directions

Prepare the quinoa according to packet directions. You should generally prepare the quinoa over low heat until the water is fully absorbed. Now make the dressing.

Add one clove of finely chopped garlic with a pinch of salt as you chop the parsley. Add the parsley to the garlic then add 3-4 tablespoons olive oil, mix and set aside.

Now add rest of the olive oil and chopped garlic to a large pan. When the garlic starts sizzling, add the kale and one pinch of salt, and sauté until it wilts a little bit. As you wait for the kale to soften, shred the roast chicken.

Just before you serve, halve the avocado, remove its pit; peel it using a spoon and set aside. Now add the kale, shredded chicken, quinoa and avocado to three plates and drizzle with the garlic-parsley dressing. Finish the dish off with black pepper and enjoy!

Cauliflower "Rice" Stir-Fry

Serves 2-3

Ingredients

1 cup cauliflower florets (one large head)

1/2 sliced red onion, divided

Coarse salt, to taste

1/2 tablespoon minced fresh ginger

1 cup broccoli florets

1/4 red bell pepper, stemmed, seeded, and diced

1 tablespoon shelled pumpkin seeds

1 tablespoon coconut or extra-virgin olive oil, divided

2 minced cloves garlic, divided

1/8 cup low-sodium vegetable broth

1/2 thinly sliced small red chili

1/2 julienned large carrot

Juice of 1/4 lemon

1 tablespoon fresh cilantro leaves

Directions

Add the cauliflower to your food processor and pulse until finely chopped.

Slice the red onion and two minced cloves of garlic and cook, while stirring, until it becomes tender, for about 6 minutes. Now add the cauliflower and season the dish with salt.

Add in the vegetable broth bit by bit, cover and cook until the broth evaporates and the cauliflower is tender, for about six minutes. Transfer everything to a bowl and cover.

Wipe your pan and heat a tablespoon of oil over medium-high heat. Add some red onion and cook while stirring for about five minutes, until tender. Now add some ginger, garlic and chili and continue cooking for another minute,

Now add the carrot, broccoli florets and bell pepper, and cook, while stirring, until tender, for five or so minutes. Season the dish with some salt, remove from the heat and add the lemon juice.

Now top cauliflower for each serving with vegetables, and sprinkle with one tablespoon of cilantro and one tablespoon of pumpkin seeds.

Serve and enjoy!

Honey & Soy Glazed Radishes

Serves 2-3

Ingredients

1 bunch of radishes, with greens

1/4 cup honey

1 tablespoon unseasoned rice vinegar

2 fried eggs for serving

1 1/2 tablespoons olive oil

2 tablespoons soy sauce

1 cup cooked white rice

Directions

Separate the greens and radishes and chop the former roughly. Slice the larger radishes in half; the smaller ones can remain whole.

Add the oil to a large skillet and heat it over medium-high heat. Now add the radishes and cook until they turn brown a bit, and are crisp tender, this should take about ten minutes.

Pour in the honey and lower the heat to medium. Cook until the radishes are glazed, for between 3 and 5 minutes. Add the soy sauce and cook until the dish becomes syrupy; this should take about 5 minutes. Add in the radish greens and rice vinegar while stirring, increase the heat to high and keep cooking until the greens wilt and most of the liquid evaporates.

Serve with rice and fried eggs.

Enjoy!

Stir-Fried Chicken With Corn and Millet

Serves 2

Ingredients

3 ounces boneless, skinless chicken thighs cut into 1-inch pieces

Salt and Pepper to taste

2 cloves garlic, sliced thinly

2/3 cup cooked millet

1/4 lime, juiced

½ tablespoon olive oil

½ cup fresh corn kernels (from 1 small ear)

2 tablespoons fresh parsley, chopped

1/4 ripe avocado, chopped into 1/2-inch pieces

Directions

Season the chicken with pepper and salt on all sides. Set your skillet over medium heat, and add the olive oil.

When it heats up, add the garlic and chicken and cook for about 4 minutes, or until the chicken is well cooked through without forgetting to stir occasionally.

Add the corn and cook, stirring often, for about two more minutes, or until it just begins to soften.

Add the millet, juice, parsley and cook, while stirring, until the dish is heated through. Add the avocado on top and serve.

Enjoy!

Chicken Chili

Serves 2

Ingredients

1 tablespoon olive oil

1 garlic clove, minced

1/4 teaspoon chili powder

1/2 teaspoon kosher salt

1/2 teaspoon dried basil

Shredded cheddar cheese, optional for topping

1 cup chopped onion (1/2 small onion)

1 small red pepper, cored, seeded, and largely diced

1/4 teaspoon ground cumin

1 15-ounce can of diced tomatoes

1 chicken breast, cooked and chopped

Sour cream, optional for topping

Directions

Heat the olive oil over medium low heat and cook the onions in the oil for between 8 and 10 minutes; the onions should be translucent. Add the garlic and continue cooking for one more minute. Add the chili powder, red peppers, salt and cook for another minute.

Add the diced tomatoes, dried basil to the pan and bring to a boil. Lower the heat to low and simmer, uncovered, for 15 minutes.

Now add the cooked, chopped chicken to the pan and simmer for 5 more minutes. Divide the dish between two bowls and top each with sour cream and shredded cheddar cheese if you like.

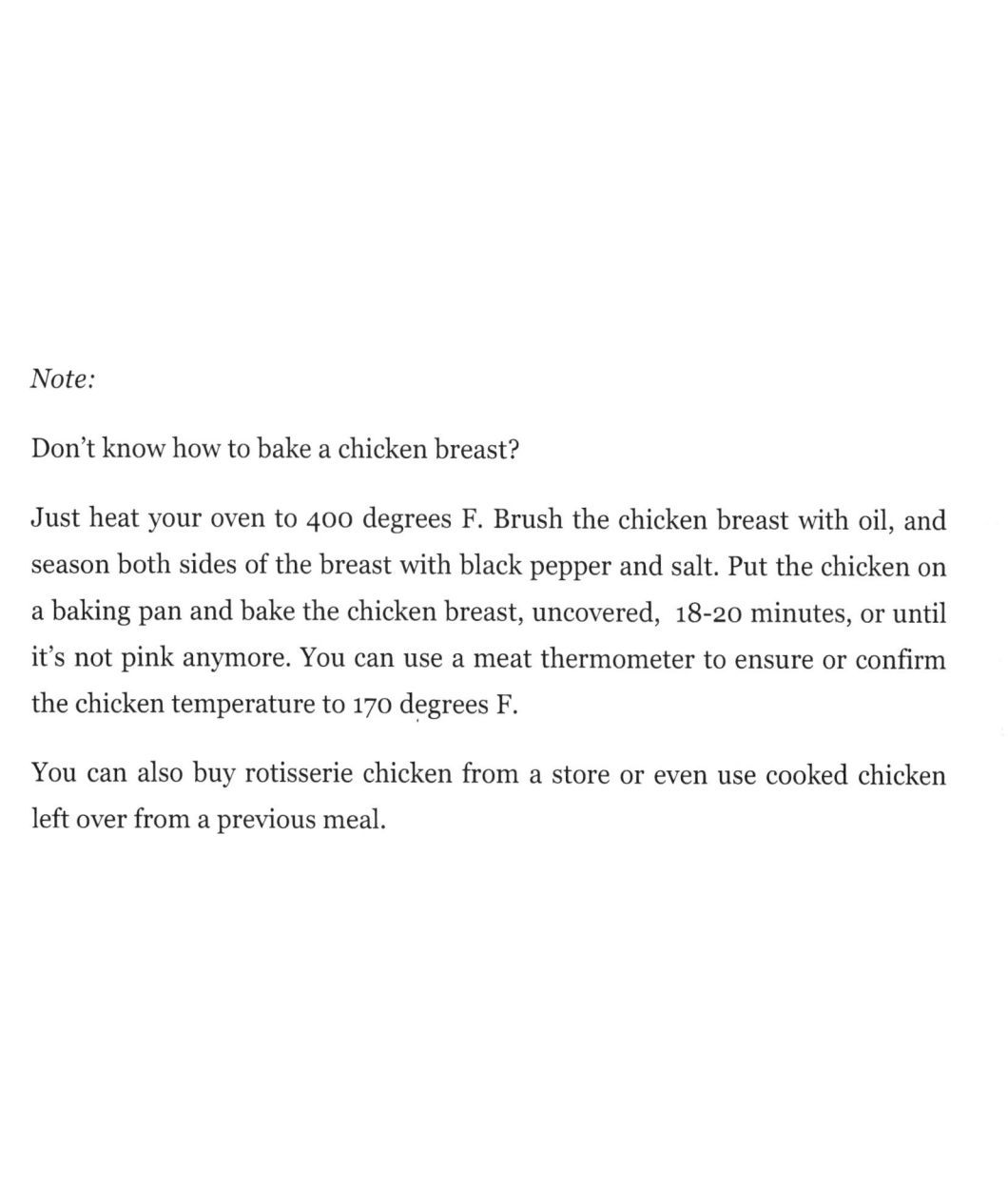

Note:

Don't know how to bake a chicken breast?

Just heat your oven to 400 degrees F. Brush the chicken breast with oil, and season both sides of the breast with black pepper and salt. Put the chicken on a baking pan and bake the chicken breast, uncovered, 18-20 minutes, or until it's not pink anymore. You can use a meat thermometer to ensure or confirm the chicken temperature to 170 degrees F.

You can also buy rotisserie chicken from a store or even use cooked chicken left over from a previous meal.

Easy Shrimp Scampi

Serves 2

Ingredients

1/4 pound shrimp, about 6

2-3 cloves garlic, minced

3 tablespoons cream

1/8 teaspoon crushed red pepper flakes, optional

Salt and pepper

1/4 cup reserved pasta water

1 large shallot, minced

2 tablespoons butter

Splash of white wine, optional

Parmesan cheese, optional

Spaghetti

Directions

Prepare the pasta according to the box instructions and reserve a bit of the cooking water for the sauce later. Drain the pasta and set aside.

Now mince the shallots and garlic and clean up the shrimp if you need to.

Set a pot over medium heat and add butter. When it's hot and melted, add the cleaned shrimp and cook for 1 minute and 30 seconds each side. Add the garlic and shallots and cook for 30 more seconds until soft. Add the crushed red pepper and a splash of wine, and be careful not to overcook them. Pour the cream on the shrimp while stirring; in the end, the sauce should be slightly reduced.

Add the pasta to the pot and stir well. Season with pepper and salt and if you find the sauce too thick, add some reserved pasta water to thin it out. Just avoid making it too thin.

Serve immediately and enjoy!

Skillet Chicken Thighs with Potato, Apple, and Spinach

Serves 1-2

Ingredients

1 small chicken thigh (bone-in, skin-on, about 4 ounces)

Salt and pepper to taste

1 medium russet potato, cut into 1/2-inch cubes

1 teaspoon fresh sage, chopped

1teaspoon canola oil

1 small Fuji apple (or any other variety), cored and cut into 6 wedges

1/2 cup packed baby spinach

Directions

Preheat your oven to 400 degrees F.

Season the chicken with pepper and salt liberally. Set an oven-safe skillet over medium heat, add the oil and heat it.

Add the chicken with the skin side down, and cook until it crisps a bit, and some fat is rendered; this should take about 3 minutes. Now add apple, potato and sage. Toss it to coat and arrange the apple and potato nicely around the pan with the chicken.

Transfer the skillet to the oven and roast for 15 minutes. Flip the chicken and roast for ten more minutes, until the apples and potatoes are soft, and the chicken cooks through, without any pink in the middle.

Take back the skillet to the stovetop set over medium-low heat. Take the chicken out, add the spinach and toss with apples and potatoes to wilt.

Top the vegetable mixture with the chicken to serve.

Jerk Tempeh Salad with Mango Salsa

Serves 3

Ingredients

<u>For the mango salsa:</u>

1/2 cup diced mango

1/8 cup diced red onion

2 ½ cloves garlic, minced (1 tablespoon)

1/2 teaspoon rice vinegar

1/2 red bell pepper, diced

1/8 cup chopped cilantro

1/4- inch knob ginger, grated

Salt

<u>For the salad:</u>

3/4 cup cooked red kidney beans (1 can drained and rinsed)

1/2 cup chopped green cabbage

1/8 cup chopped cilantro

1/2 cup packed baby spinach, roughly chopped

1/2 cup cooked brown rice

Salt and pepper

<u>For the Jerk Tempeh:</u>

1 (4-ounce) block tempeh

1 tablespoon jerk seasoning (store-bought or homemade — recipe below)

1 tablespoon coconut oil, melted (plus additional to coat pan)

Directions

To prepare the mango salsa, simply add the mango, red onion, ginger, rice vinegar, red bell pepper, salt, garlic and cilantro to a bowl and mix until well integrated. Set aside until ready to serve.

To make the salad, simply mix the baby spinach, kidney beans, cooked brown rice, green cabbage, cilantro, pepper and salt and set aside until you are ready to serve it.

To prepare the tempeh, just brush all the sides of the tempeh with coconut oil and then coat with the jerk seasoning. Coat a skillet and set it over medium heat. Add the tempeh block and cook for four minutes or until the bottom area becomes crisp and brown. Flip and cook on the other side for four minutes or until the other side is browned and crisp. Grab a spatula and transfer it to a chopping board. Slice it into pieces.

To serve, divide the tempeh pieces and salad between three plates (or one plate and store the rest if you're alone) and spoon the mango salsa on top. Serve with the rest of the salsa if you want.

Note:

If you want, you can make the salad, tempeh and salsa up to two days in advance; just ensure you store the mango salsa separately to avoid sogginess.

How to prepare the Jerk seasoning

This jerk seasoning serves up to 6 plates

Ingredients

1 tablespoon garlic powder

1 tablespoon dry thyme

2 teaspoons allspice

½ teaspoon crushed red pepper

½ teaspoon ground ginger

1 tablespoon cayenne pepper (see note)

2 teaspoons salt

½ teaspoon black pepper

½ teaspoon ground cinnamon

Directions

Stir the cayenne pepper, garlic powder, allspice, thyme, black pepper, cinnamon, ginger, crushed red pepper and salt.

Use the mixture for meat, poultry, tempeh, tofu or fish.

Remember:

If you want a milder flavor, you can omit or reduce the cayenne pepper.

Store in a dry, airtight container.

Snacks and Desserts

Chocolate Rice Pudding

Serves 2

Ingredients

1/4 cup long grain rice

1/8 teaspoon salt

1/4 teaspoon vanilla extract (may also use Crème de Cacao instead)

2 tablespoons sugar

1/2 tablespoon cocoa powder

2 tablespoons semisweet chocolate chips

1 cup milk

Directions

Add the milk, rice, salt and sugar to a saucepan and set it over medium heat. Bring to a boil; stir occasionally until the rice becomes tender, and the pudding is thick. This should take about 20 minutes.

Remove the saucepan from the heat and add the vanilla and cocoa powder to the mixture.

Now add the chocolate chips to the mixture until they melt fully.

Transfer the mixture to your bowl and let it cool for 10 minutes; serve warm and enjoy!

Homemade Papaya Fruit Roll Ups

Serves 2

Ingredients

200g papaya cubed

Juice of a quarter a lemon

30 ml maple syrup

Directions

Add the papaya, maple syrup and lemon juice to a blender and process until smooth.

Preheat your oven to 170 degrees F. Line a baking tray with parchment paper. Pour the mixture on the tray and spread it out as thinly as you can, using a spatula.

Bang the tray on a flat surface carefully, to ensure the mix flattens evenly.

Put it in the oven and let it bake for 4-5 hours, or until it is firm to the touch.

Let it cool and then put it on the parchment and cut into strips. Roll and tie using a string.

Enjoy and store the remaining roll-ups in an air tight container for not more than one week.

No Bake Key Lime Pies

Serves 8

Ingredients

2 large eggs

1/2 cup key lime juice

1 package Keebler Ready Crust Mini Graham Cracker

1 fresh key lime, cut into slices

Mint leaves

2/3 cup granulated sugar

1/4 cup butter

1 cup cool whip

6 raspberries

Directions

Add water to a saucepan and heat it over a stove to a low boil. Add the eggs. Key lime juice and sugar to a glass bowl and whisk them until well integrated.

Put the bowl on top of the simmering water carefully, making sure it fits well so that the steam does not escape.

Stir the mixture constantly until it attains 180 degrees and becomes desirably thick. Remove it from the heat and add in the butter while stirring until smooth. Add the key lime curd into the mini graham cracker crusts in even proportions and press a little piece of plastic wrap on each pie on the surface. Put it in your fridge until chilled.

Remove the plastic wrap and using a piping bag and an icing tip to swirl the whip over the pies.

Now top with raspberry, key lime slice and mint leaves.

Serve and enjoy!

Peanut Butter Balls

Serves 3

Ingredients

4 teaspoons peanut butter

1/4 cup (slightly heaping) powdered sugar

1 tablespoon softened butter

1/4 cup semisweet chocolate chips

Directions

Stir the softened butter and peanut butter together until well blended and smooth. Add in powdered sugar while stirring and roll the dough into three balls. Put the chocolate chips in the microwave to warm, and coat the peanut butter balls in chocolate. Allow the chocolate to set and harden slightly. If you are impatient, you can stick them in the fridge.

Enjoy!

Tasty Scone

Serves 2

Ingredients

1/3 cup flour

1/4 teaspoon salt

1 tablespoon cold butter, cut into small cubes

2 tablespoons mix-in of choice, such as cranberry or walnut

1/2 teaspoon baking powder

1 tablespoon sugar

2 1/2 tablespoons milk

Directions

Preheat your oven to 450 degrees F. You can use a small food processor to break up the butter into flour or simply use your fingers.

Add the sugar, salt and baking powder to a food processor and the processed butter. Next, add in the milk and mix-ins and process until you see the dough pulling away from the mixer's side. This should take a short while.

Pull the dough away from the blade carefully and shape it into two circles ensuring that the circles are roughly ½ inch in thickness. Bake on a piece of parchment paper at 450 for about 8-10 minutes, or until golden brown. Let it cool a bit before you dig in.

Enjoy!

Chocolate Chip Cookies

Serves 1-2

Ingredients

2 tablespoons of butter

1 tablespoon of granulated sugar

1/4 teaspoon of pure vanilla extract

1/4 teaspoon of baking soda

3 heaping tablespoons of semisweet chocolate chips

2 firmly packed tablespoons of dark brown sugar

Pinch of kosher salt

1 egg yolk

1/4 cup of all-purpose flour

Directions

Preheat your oven to 350 degrees F and then line a baking sheet with parchment paper as it heats up. Add butter to a microwavable bowl and heat it until it just begins melting and is soft. Using your hand, mix the vanilla, salt, sugars and the softened butter by hand.

Add the yolk and stir once more.

Add the flour and baking soda and stir until well integrated.

Now add in the chocolate chips while stirring and make two balls; place them on a baking sheet, a few inches apart.

Bake for 8 or so minutes, or until the edges turn golden brown.

Remove the baking sheet from the oven and bang the baking sheet carefully and firmly on the counter top. Your cookie will be deflated by doing so, and it will have a perfect wrinkly appearance.

Banana Bread Mug Cake

Serves 1

Ingredients

Non-stick cooking spray

1 tablespoon plus 1 teaspoon sugar

1/8 teaspoon salt

1/8 teaspoon baking soda

1/4 teaspoon vanilla extract

1 tablespoon milk

3 tablespoons flour

2 tablespoons brown sugar

1/8 teaspoon baking powder

1 egg

1 tablespoon vegetable oil

1 ripe banana mashed

Directions

Coat your microwavable safe mug with cooking spray. Add the flour, baking powder, soda, salt and sugar to a mug or bowl and whisk. Add the egg and continue whisking until just integrated. Add in the milk, oil, mashed banana and vanilla while mixing.

Pop the mixture into the microwave for about 3 minutes; you can check after 1 ½ minutes for doneness.

Like most things that come out of a microwave, the bread will be very hot in the inside when you first take it out, so give it a couple of minutes to cool.

Enjoy!

Baked Brie

Serves 2

Ingredients

1 can refrigerated crescent roll dough

4 ounces Brie cheese (I cut out my 16 ounce wheel of Brie into wedges, which makes it very simple to portion out)

8 teaspoons strawberry jam

Directions

Start by unrolling the crescent roll dough and scooping out one teaspoon of strawberry jam onto all triangles.

Put half an ounce of the cheese on the jam- you can cut 4 wedges in half.

Wrap up the dough edges around the cheese and jam; cup your palms around the dough to create a ball. Ensure all the edges are well sealed- you don't want to lose a lot of jam and cheese.

Bake it for about 13-15 minutes at 400 degrees, until golden brown.

Enjoy right away!

Chocolate Peanut Butter Mug Cake

Serves 1

Ingredients

2 tablespoons butter

1/2 teaspoon vanilla

2 tablespoons sugar

3 tablespoons cocoa powder

1/8 teaspoon baking powder

2 tablespoons Peanut Butter

1 egg

2 tablespoons flour

1/8 teaspoon salt

3 tablespoons chocolate chips

Directions

Melt the butter in a bowl in the microwave. Add in the peanut butter and combine properly. Add the sugar, egg and vanilla to a mug and mix together until well combined.

Separately, mix the flour, baking powder, salt and cocoa and add to the mug. Add in the butter/peanut butter mixture to the same mug and combine well. Add in the chocolate chips while stirring and put the mixture in the microwave.

Let it heat up until the desired doneness is attained, for 1-2 minutes. Remember that microwaves are different, so you have to do a little experiment while adjusting the time as required. I only do it for one minute. Top it with hot fudge and peanut butter pie mousse below:

Peanut Butter Pie Mousse

1 tablespoon cream cheese, softened

1/2 teaspoon vanilla

1 tablespoon powdered sugar

1 tablespoon Peanut Butter

2 tablespoons cool whip

Hot Fudge

Directions

Combine the vanilla, peanut butter and cream cheese well and fold in the whipped cream. Sift the powdered sugar as you add in- you can use a fork- and fold it in as well; just try to avoid over-stirring it.

Jumbo Fluffy Sugar Cookie

Yields one large cookie

Ingredients

2 tablespoons butter, room temperature

2 tablespoons beaten egg

6 tablespoons flour

1/4 teaspoon kosher salt

4 tablespoons granulated sugar

1/2 teaspoon vanilla

1/4 teaspoon baking soda

1/4 teaspoon cream of tartar

Directions

Preheat your oven to 350 degrees F. Line a little cookie sheet with parchment paper. Add the sugar and butter to a medium-sized bowl and stir well until creamed. Add in the vanilla and egg and combine.

Add in the baking soda, flour, salt and cream of tartar while stirring until well combined.

Put the dough in the middle of the cookie sheet and bake for between 13 and 15 minutes, or until the edges turn brown.

Let it cool for some time on a wire rack.

Enjoy!

Greek Tart with Apricot Jam

Serves 8

Ingredients

300 grams apricot jam

2 teaspoons baking powder

2 eggs

3/4 cup coconut sugar

500 grams coconut flour

280 grams Butter

Directions

Using a mixer, whisk melted butter and then add in eggs and sugar. Add in the flour gradually until you make soft dough. Store the dough in the fridge for around 30 minutes.

After the 30 minutes, remove the dough from the fridge, roll out 2/3 of the dough in greased or buttered tart pan, placing it all way around the pan sides. Press it gently to evenly to cover the bottom and sides.

Roll out the extra dough into 1/2cm thick roll and then cut it into strips.

Evenly spread the jam and then cover using the dough strips. Bake it at 180 C for 45 minutes.

Peanut Butter Smoothie

Serves 1

Ingredients

Pinch of salt

1 pinch stevia

¼ teaspoon cinnamon

2 tablespoons creamy peanut butter

1 cup coconut milk, unsweetened

1 scoop chocolate whey protein

1 tablespoon cocoa powder, unsweetened

Directions

Combine the ingredients in a blender and blend until smooth.

Serve and enjoy.

Sample Meal Plan

Week 1

	Sunday	Monday	Tuesday	Wednesday	Thursday	Friday	Saturday
7.00 am	Maple Oatmeal with Sweet Potato	Blueberry-Almond Oatmeal	Banana and Almond Porridge	Waffles with Nut Butter and Bananas	Toast with Yogurt and Smoked Salmon	Fluffy Waffle	Protein Pancake
9.30 am	5-Minute Mug Breakfast	Egg Muffin Sandwiches	Deep Purple Smoothie	savory microwave breakfast mug	breakfast sandwich	Overnight chia oatmeal in a mason jar	Breakfast Burrito
12.30 pm	Quick & Easy Cucumber Salad	Angel Hair Casserole	Caprese Fusilli	Mexican Quinoa Stuffed Peppers	Smoked mackerel & leek hash	Blackened salmon fajitas	Microwave Quiche in a Mug
3.30 pm	Left-overs	Left-overs	Left-overs	Left-overs	Left-overs	Left-overs	Left-overs
6.30 pm	Miso Udon	Smoky Artichoke-Sardine Salad	Tutti-Frutti Muesli	Pork Chop with Pineapple Salsa	Poke Avocado Bowl	Smoked mackerel & leek hash	Creamy pork chop with mustard and apples
8.00 pm	Moroccan-Spiced Cod with Cauliflower	Beet Salad on a Stick	Grilled Garlic Shrimp Skewers	Sweet and Spicy Tuna Salad	Charred Corn and Zucchini Salad	Lemony Artichoke and Quinoa Salad	Chocolate Rice Pudding

Week 2

	Sunday	Monday	Tuesday	Wednesday	Thursday	Friday	Saturday
7.00 am	Pancakes	Banana nut overnight oats	Easy Summer Breakfast Parfaits	Egg Wraps	PB&J toast	5-minute honey yogurt quinoa parfait	Breakfast Banana Splits
9.30 am	French Toast in A Cup	Mocha Breakfast Shake	Italian Baked Eggs	Quick Bowl of Polenta	Egg-in-a-hole	Apple Pie Oatmeal	Honey Lime Quinoa Fruit Salad
12.30 pm	Broccoli Tots	Quinoa Fajita Burritos	Vegetable Lo Mein	Grazer's Lunch	Veggie Fried Rice	Vegetarian bolognaise hand pies	Mini schnitzels with garlic sauce
3.30 pm	Recipe of choice	Left-overs	Recipe of choice	Left-overs	Recipe of choice	Left-overs	Recipe of choice
6.30 pm	Grilled Zucchini Hummus Wrap	Tex-Mex Quinoa Brown Rice	Lighter Pea Carbonara	Salmon & couscous	Easy 5-Ingredient Corn Soup	Caramelized onions on the grill	Sheet-Pan Chicken Fajitas
8.00 pm	Kale, Quinoa, Avocado & Roast Chicken Salad	Cauliflower "Rice" Stir-Fry	Honey & Soy Glazed Radishes	Stir-Fried Chicken With Corn and Millet	Chicken Chili Recipe For One	Easy Shrimp Scampi For One	Skillet Chicken Thighs with Potato, Apple, and Spinach

Week 3

	Sunday	Monday	Tuesday	Wednesday	Thursday	Friday	Saturday
7.00 am	Ricotta Toast with Honey and Pistachios	My Go-to Smoothie Bowl	Breakfast Tacos	Oatmeal Power Bowl	The Best Avocado Toast and Egg Recipe	Healthy Berry Yogurt Smoothie	Savory Oatmeal with Cheddar and Fried Egg
9.30 am	Recipe of choice	Recipe of choice	Left-overs	Left-overs	Left-overs	Recipe of choice	Left-overs
12.30 pm	Avocado, Mango, and Toasted Seed Salad	Avocado, Mango, and Toasted Seed Salad	Mini Katsudon	Mini satay chicken skewers	Egg Fried Rice in a Mug	Egg and Potato Salad Pita	Potato Soup In A Mug
3.30 pm	Left-overs	Left-overs	Left-overs	Left-overs	Left-overs	Left-overs	Left-overs
6.30 pm	Jerk Tempeh Salad with Mango Salsa	Smoky Artichoke-Sardine Salad	Tutti-Frutti Muesli	Pork Chop with Pineapple Salsa	Poke Avocado Bowl	Maple Oatmeal with Sweet Potato	Creamy pork chop with mustard and apples
8.00 pm	Moroccan-Spiced Cod with Cauliflower	Beet Salad on a Stick	Grilled Garlic Shrimp Skewers	Charred Corn and Zucchini Salad	Lemony Artichoke and Quinoa Salad	Chocolate Rice Pudding	Sweet and Spicy Tuna Salad

In case you're wondering, you can have the snacks anytime during the day.

Again, this table is just a simplified example of how you can organize your meals throughout the week. You do not have to cook all day. Most of the meals can have more than one serving, which means that you can store and eat them whenever your plan stipulates. For instance, you can prepare maple oatmeal with sweet potato recipe and divide the food among three and four meals to eat within a period of two –three days.

Lastly, you can tweak the table to fit your daily schedule, family size, taste or anything like that. You should eventually have a meal plan that suits you perfectly.

Conclusion

We have come to the end of the book. Thank you for reading and congratulations for reading until the end.

If you found the book valuable, can you recommend it to others? One way to do that is to post a review on Amazon.

Click here to leave a review for this book on Amazon!

Thank you and good luck!